Writing Flash Fiction

The Essential Guide to Professional Flash Fiction

(Tested Story Starters for Short Stories and Flash Fiction)

Jennifer Richards

Published By **Simon Dough**

Jennifer Richards

All Rights Reserved

Writing Flash Fiction: The Essential Guide to Professional Flash Fiction (Tested Story Starters for Short Stories and Flash Fiction)

ISBN 978-1-77485-943-8

No part of this guidebook shall be reproduced in any form without permission in writing from the publisher except in the case of brief quotations embodied in critical articles or reviews.

Legal & Disclaimer

The information contained in this ebook is not designed to replace or take the place of any form of medicine or professional medical advice. The information in this ebook has been provided for educational & entertainment purposes only.

The information contained in this book has been compiled from sources deemed reliable, and it is accurate to the best of the Author's knowledge; however, the Author cannot guarantee its accuracy and validity and cannot be held liable for any errors or omissions. Changes are periodically made to this book. You must consult your doctor or get professional medical advice before using any of the suggested remedies, techniques, or information in this book.

Upon using the information contained in this book, you agree to hold harmless the Author from and against any damages, costs, and expenses, including any legal fees potentially resulting from the application of any of the information provided by this guide. This disclaimer applies to any damages or injury caused by the use and application, whether directly or indirectly, of any advice or information presented, whether for breach of contract, tort, negligence, personal injury, criminal intent, or under any other cause of action.

You agree to accept all risks of using the information presented inside this book. You need to consult a professional medical practitioner in order to ensure you are both able and healthy enough to participate in this program.

Table of contents

Chapter 1: How Short Is It? 1

Chapter 2: Story Genres 5

Chapter 3: Short Story Markets 17

Chapter 4: Analysing The Markets 27

Chapter 5: Other Ways You Can Get Published 34

Chapter 6: Where Do Your Ideas Come From? 49

Chapter 7: Making A Great Introduction .61

Chapter 8: Structures And Plot 69

Chapter 9: Using Flashbacks 80

Chapter 10: Gently Does It 85

Chapter 1: How short is it?

In this chapter, we will be looking at "What is the definition of a short story?" as well as "How short can a story be?" It's Edgar Allen Poe's definition, which is often quoted. He defined a short tale as:

"A story you can read in one go."

Poe also stated, "A story shouldn't have any in it which detracts or distracts from the design." With that, I think he meant short stories shouldn't contain anything unnecessary that's not essential to the tale being told. By sticking to the points, characters should not be added to the plot. A short story should not be distracted from its goal.

Edgar Allan Poe believed that one sitting could mean that a story could take anywhere from 30 minutes to an entire hour or more. Our attention spans are decreasing these days. We are much more comfortable viewing brief clips of film or reading concise, summarized news articles on the TV and the internet. Short stories have become less popular due to this. A short story will now likely be something that can easily be read in between five and thirty minutes.

There are three main lengths of stories that are most popular in UK magazines: 1,000, 2000, and 3,000. While editors might prefer to publish longer pieces of writing, it is not uncommon for the story to be serialized in more than one issue. The United States has many magazine editors who will take longer stories with 7,500 to 10,000 words. Stories of 1,000, 2, 000, or 3,000 words are popular and are most likely be given a home by an editor. But, the magazine's requirements will dictate how long you write your story. To put it another way, if your goal is to sell your story you need to write it as long as the editor requires.

You don't need to write a 4,500 word story if the magazine that you're writing for has only 2,000 word stories. To be successful, you must research your market well and create stories that meet the editor's specifications. We'll be discussing story markets in greater detail in a future chapter. I'm referring to where you plan to sell your book.

Before I move on, I wanted to briefly mention that short stories can be sold in places that have less than 1,000 words. These are sometimes called short stories or flash fiction. The most popular word count for shortshorts is 500 words. There are many online places that publish these stories. Some writers I know have even collected several short-shorts together to create an eBook collection.

Then, there are the 50- and 60-word stories. While I sold many of these stories to UK magazines in past years, they seem to have lost some of their popularity recently. They are still popular, especially online. Here's one I wrote some time back:

Dylan, her great-grandson, glowed across the assembly hall. Michelle was proud of her moment. Michelle Alderton had never graduated from university. She listened patiently and waited for the roll call to be completed. Dylan managed a discrete waving. It came. "... Michelle Alderton was awarded the Bachelor in Arts Degree. Michelle smiled proudly when she received her degree.

How long did it take you to read that article? 20 seconds? 30 maybe? These short stories can be small but they are still complete stories in their own right, often with a twist. They are fun to write and can be challenging to fit into the tight word count. It's a great exercise in editing.

Make 60-word stories about yourself and see what they do.

Chapter 2: Story genres

Now that we've discussed the brief story and the word count required to complete one, let's dive deeper and look at the different story types.

Before we get started, I would like you to set aside this book and grab some paper. Write as many stories as you can. At least five story types should be on your list. When you're finished, go back to this page.

*****

Did you find the task simple? Although you probably thought of at least three to four stories quickly, I suspect that the last two on your list took a bit more time. I have fourteen types of short stories on my list, but I have had more time to think about it. There are more story types than I have time to add. And you might have something on your list that doesn't show up on mine.

So, now I am going to go through my list (in no particular order) and compare it with yours. Each story type should be considered and compared to your own.

Romance: These are stories of love between two adults.

Other relationships stories: These stories include stories about relationships that don't involve romance. It could be a relationship between a parent and child, siblings or friends, a boss and an employee, or next-door-neighbours.

Twist endings/Twist in the Tale Stories: These stories are unexpected or surprise endings and can even contain a "double twist" to add more surprise. O Henry and Roald Dahl are two writers who are known for this type stories. Twist stories have a long history of popularity with readers. There are plenty markets for them.

Historical: These are stories that take place in the distant future. It could be the Middle Ages. Tudor England. The American War of Independence. Or any other period of history.

Sometimes, historical stories are combined with other story genres like historical romance and historic crime.

Nostalgia - These stories are very similar to historical ones, but are usually set in the near future, almost always within living memory. It could be about a child growing-up during the Second World War. These stories are a great way to evoke fond memories.

Humour: These don't have to be comedies. They are more observations about life. Many magazines appreciate stories with a touch of humor, so it's well worth the effort.

Ghost stories: Ghost Stories never seem out of fashion. There are chilling ghost stories which send chills down the spine. There are also stories about benevolent, friendly, or even incompetent haunts. The magazine you aim for will determine what kind of ghost stories you can write.

Crime stories: These are always very popular. They are sometimes referred as police procedural stories and revolve around the ultimate crime: murder.

I've separated these mystery stories because although they may involve a crime, they are usually "cosy" crimes. The investigation is usually carried out by amateur sleuths and takes place in a beautiful or intimate setting. Some magazines won't publish crime stories but will accept mysteries. There is an important difference between the stories.

Horror: An immensely popular genre. Stephen King, the 'King' in horror fiction, published several collections including Nightmares and Dreamscapes and Full Dark, No Stars. His work can be a great source of inspiration for writers.

Science fiction is another very popular genre. If you're interested in creating your own worlds, times, and a new race of beings with your imagination, these stories are for you.

Fantasy: Fantasy stories are often associated with science fiction. They feature imaginary worlds, creatures, and sometimes include magic, special powers, myth, and other elements. They can take readers and their imaginations almost anywhere.

Erotica: Erotica can be a difficult genre to write. But, there is a lot of demand. There are many opportunities to publish short stories in the erotica category on Kindle Direct Publishing. It can be very lucrative if this is something you enjoy. Remember that you have the option to publish your work under a pseudonym (or penname) if desired.

Children's stories: Short stories are a great way to get your message across. But the core elements of story, such plot, characterisation, etc., are the same. Understanding your market, knowing the appeal of your target audience and choosing the language and subject that is appropriate for the age groups you're writing for, are all key factors.

There we are. These are the genres I have compiled for you to consider writing stories about. It's up to you to decide which genre is appealing to you. You will enjoy writing if you find a niche that interests and appeals to you.

To find the story genre that suits you best, I would like you to complete a writing assignment. This exercise starts on page 2.

The exercise is split into three parts. The first part is about the type of stories you enjoy reading. Next, you'll do an exercise that uses the right side (creative) of your mind. Next, you will complete another exercise using your left (creative side) brain. Finally, you will use the results to help you generate story ideas.

Then, complete the exercise. Next, we'll move to the next chapter. This chapter will be a closer examination of short story markets and what it takes to find them.

Writing exercise: What's your story type?

Question 1: What book are you currently reading?

Notify the title of everything you are reading right now. It could be a book, a magazine, a poetry collection, or a novel.

Question 2: As a reader, which fictional stories are your favourite?

Check as many categories as possible from the list.

* Romance

* Family/other relationships

* Tales with twists

* Historical fiction

* Nostalgic stories

* Ghost stories

* Crime stories

* The cozy crime of mystery stories

* Humorous stories

* Horror

* Science Fiction

* Fantasy stories

* Erotica

* Children's stories

Next, take a look at this list, but this one as a writer. Note the story categories that interest you. It doesn't matter if you already ticked that category.

Drawing on the right-side of your brain

I'd love you to try a random writing activity. This will encourage you to think from the right side (creative) of your brain. Do not think about these questions too much. Simply write down anything that comes to you, no matter how odd or unlikely.

These are your notes. You are the only one who can see them, and you don't want anyone else to.

Begin by making a list.

It could be a place you know well or one that you would like to return to. You might also choose a specific venue such as a bookstore, cafe or auction house. Write until you feel exhausted.

Next, take three deep breathing in and close your eyes. Next, close your eyes. Now, take three deep, exhaling breaths.

This may sound bizarre, but you should accept it. This is how you will get to the core of your subconscious. The words should flow naturally, so don't worry about them. You must not give your left brain the opportunity to censor what words you write.

Once you're done with the list write two more words that you can associate with each word. It may seem odd at first, but keep at it. This could be, for example, if you wrote "dogs" in one of the words, you can add "bite" or "fear" to the words. Or fur and?loyalty '.... If you put a cup in the first list, additional words could include 'tea or crack', or porcelain or â€" all of these. If you wrote down the word "cottage", you could add 'thatched,' or haunted' to it.

Draw on the left side.

Now your left brain can have a voice (let's face the fact that it has probably been trying in vain for the last five seconds).).

Logically think about all the things you have a lot of knowledge about that you feel confident writing about. You could list, for example, "being a parent", 'driving your car', "owning cats" or "commuting to the workplace by train". It doesn't have to mean anything significant; just something you're familiar with could add a touch of reality to any story.

All this together

We will now bring all of these lists together.

Take a look at all the writings you have done and find any common words or topics. These are the areas you will feel most confident writing about.

Make sure to link the words in your lists. Then, think about how you could use the words in a story. You might think of how you could tie the two elements together, for example, if your list included 'owning dog' and "commuting home to work" on another. Maybe your main character's workplace is having a 'bring-your-dog-to-work day' and he wants to take part, but he's not sure how his dog will cope with travelling by train. What will happen when the boss's pug-loving, scruffy cross-breed terrier arrives at his office? This is likely to be a humorous tale, don't ya think?

Now, look at the things that only appear once on your settings lists and consider how you can use them as story ideas. You might write "a rugged, wind whipped coastline" on your settings lists, and live in a small, rural city. Ask yourself why you have that item on your list. Is there something you yearn to be near the sea? You might be inspired to write about someone who lives by the coast.

You may need a bit more imagination to create a seaside story than you would for one about the city. It's easier to write about what you are familiar with and it can be more authentic. There is nothing stopping you from researching a topic, setting, or occupation and writing about it. This is no different from writing about historical or fantasyland settings. It just takes some imagination and careful research. Finally, if you notice things that are not on your list but intrigue you, think about these:

*How did those items end up on the list?

* What significance they might have (if any)

* Where (if ever) they might lead to you in terms of telling a story.

You don't have to worry if things you wrote don't make sense even after you've analyzed them. Many of the things you struggled to understand when you first wrote them down will become obvious later. Sometimes even the most absurd concepts can turn into really great story ideas. It's not difficult to dismiss the seemingly unpromising ideas and use them as a springboard for more interesting stories.

Keep these lists updated. Every now and again, update these lists or create new ones. To find inspiration and story ideas when you're stuck, pull out your list. Your lists should guide you to the most suitable story genres and help to decide what type of stories to create.

Chapter 3: Short Story Markets

In this section, we will discuss one of your most important factors in author success: writing stories that suit the market you are targeting. This section will explain why it's important to know your market before you write. Additionally, I will be asking you for help in choosing a short story market.

To market...

There are generally two types:

* People who simply write for fun and don't intend to publish their work.

* people who are interested in making a living from writing and seeing their work published.

The first kind of writer is most definitely not in the minority. My opinion is that even those who only write for fun would love to see their work published.

Writing a story can be difficult. Sometimes it can be like pulling teeth. Writers don't put their heart into this process to get their work out there. A majority of writers wish to see their work published. They want readers to enjoy their stories.

Writing is a business.

Planning for success requires that you view writing as a business. Here are some ways to avoid writing stories.

1. Write a story. Spend hours creating and editing.

2. It is worth looking for someone who would be willing to buy it.

You never know when you'll be paid generously for your work. Or, even more likely, you will end up with a story nobody wants. This will result in a product that no one wants. This is how it looks:

You are considering starting a company to make footwear but don't know which type of footwear you want to make. Galoshes are your dream job. You think you could do it well, and you have all of the tools you need to make a high-quality galosh. If you were enthusiastic but not very practical, you might jump in to galosh making. After producing thousands of galoshes of dark green color, you can start to search for dealers to sell them. If no one wanted your product, how would you feel? Or, if there was a shortage of galoshes for women in blue and pink sizes? There may be a market but it's small and very competitive for galoshes. What would your dark green galoshes do?

This scenario should show you that research is key to any business.

What would your plan be if there were no market for galoshes yet there's a growing need for rubber beach sandals

Do you see the point? Write a ghost story only if there is virtually no market. You will have experienced the law of supply & demand if you ever worked in the business industry. Short story writers must understand the writing markets in order to succeed. Here's how you should approach the business of writing stories.

1. Do your research on the short story markets. Spend some time reading to see what kind of stories are popular.

2. Send in a story that matches exactly the editor's requirements and send it off.

Writing is an art, however

You might find it hard to believe that you can write commercially. I hear you roar. "Writing can be an art!" It is both true and false. The act and process of creation, including the building of your story, writing it and polishing it, are all art forms. You will have to think commercially if you wish to make a living from writing.

Fashion designers design clothing using all of their artistic abilities. Fashion designers take into consideration all elements of design, colour, and then use styles and fabric imaginatively to create exactly what they are looking for. But ultimately they create a product. It can be sold because of the market.

A word to the wise

If you create a story that fits all of the guidelines for fiction in magazines, there is a chance that you might suppress your writing voice. It's vital to find your writing style and voice. It's the thing which will bring energy, life, and passion to your work.

Try to write from your heart. It is the best way you can connect with your reader. You will find that readers will sense your passion when you write.

Your editor is your customer

While it sounds a bit mercenary, thinking of your stories as products might be a good idea. But you have to make something that people want. Your target readership refers to the readers of the magazines you wish to write for. Your customers are editors for those magazines. They know what readers want, and they have to deliver it. The editors want you to provide them with stories they will enjoy. Do not send crime stories to them if they refuse to publish crime stories. You'd be shocked at the number of people who send out work randomly in vain to get it published.

Other important consideration is to only submit stories that are right-sized for the magazine to be published. An editor will limit the space that a story or stories can take up. The rest of the magazine will have features, news, advertising and other content. These generate vital income for the magazine. If they have one page to write a short story, they will want something that is about 1,000 words. A 2,500 word story would not be acceptable, even if they are the best ever. If there's not enough room for it to be printed, the magazine will not be interested.

How to find out the editors' needs

Many magazines do not accept freelance writers. Some magazines will only accept fiction submitted by authors who have been paid to do so. Some editors will accept unsolicited manuscripts but it often means that they get many. Unsolicited manuscripts go into what is known as the 'slush stack'. It's a pile of envelopes with stories that are waiting for their turn. It may be accepted by an editor if the story is liked. If not, it may be rejected.

A review of all the magazines available is the best way for short story markets to be identified. Here's how:

Research: Stop by your local bookstore or newsagent, and look at the selection of magazines. Which magazines have you seen before? Which magazines publish short fiction? You can pick up any title you don't already know and have a quick look to find out if it contains fiction. Look out for the contact details for editors. These contact details can be found on either the index page or the back cover of the magazine. The information should include whether the magazine accepts unsolicited submissions.

Read widely: What magazines do your readers read? What about short fiction? If you are only reading magazines about sports, health, beauty, horses, software, and the latest games, it is time to make some changes in your reading habits. To write short fiction, it is necessary to become familiar with the current stories being published.

It is important to obtain current copies of magazines and read them before you submit a story. Before you submit your story, read the magazine and adapt your writing style if necessary. When you're reading through the magazine, take the time to get a sense of what the average reader is like and try to create a story for them. Write something that you believe they will like. Don't write for yourself.

Listen to the work of others: Reading the work of others can help you learn so much. You don't have to read every magazine for fun. Make sure you thoroughly study each story. Consider the opening. How much dialogue are you including? What is the word count What is its subject matter and genre? Are there happy endings, twist endings, or stories that you have to decide the end? How old is each character? Are they set in the modern world or the past? Are the stories about romance or family relationships predominant? Are there ghost stories and mysteries? Are they in the first or third person? If so, what tense have they been written in (more information in a chapter).

When you're reading, think back to what we talked about in the chapter on story types.

What would you do to categorize the stories in each of these magazines? Would you enjoy writing this kind of story?

Analyse magazine: To get a better sense of target audience, take a look at other pages. What is the content of the fashion, beauty, and health news? Does it target young people, 20-somethings, and older generations? Are there ads for family holidays, or recipes for quick and easy meals for busy mothers? If there are, working women with young families would be the target audience for the magazine. The magazine's target audience is likely to be older if it contains health tips for dealing with arthritis and beauty tips for restoring your complexion. The travel pages are another example. Are the destinations exotic or inexpensive? Or are they cheap and cheerful. It is also possible to use the letters page. What stage in life or lifestyle are the letters referring to?

Writer's guidelines: A copy of the guidelines is the best way to discover what specific requirements a magazine has. These guidelines can usually be found on the magazine's website. If they are not available, you can contact the fiction editor and request that they email you one. It's important to remember that magazines can change their guidelines at any time. Therefore, it's a good idea if you regularly update yourself to ensure you keep current with all the necessary requirements.

Lists: This is a great way of finding short story markets. You can also buy The Writers & Artists Yearbook, for the UK, or Writer's Market, for North American markets. Begin to look into a few possible story markets before moving on.

Chapter 4: Analysing the Markets

Once you've begun to look at a few short story markets you can begin to think about which one appeals to you. Look on the website for a magazine where you are interested in writing. For those that do, make sure to read the guidelines carefully.

* Market specific requirements.

* Subjects that are welcomed, and those not.

* The subtle differences between magazines vary depending on the readership.

Writing for a magazine, such as Woman's Weekly or The People's Friend, is one example of the differences in UK. Let's use these magazines as an example of how stories can change from one magazine and another.

Let's take this example: A 1,000-word story about a divorced woman. Her husband was having an affair and she decided to throw him out. She has to learn how to live alone and care for her home. Although she could easily hire someone to help her with home maintenance, that would not be feasible for her. She also wants to take care of things herself. She wants to be self-sufficient. She relies on her ex-husband far too often.

OK. So, that's the basic outline of a story. It's not clear at this point what obstacles (conflicts) the protagonist will need to overcome. However, it's clear that it's not going to end in a love story. We won't introduce any handy male who is great at home-improvement. The story will tell how the protagonist copes with her new situation. It will end on a positive note. Although we haven't yet worked out the ending.

Let's stop at this point and review the idea.

Reviewing your story idea

Let's look at the facts about this idea. The People's Friend's fiction guidelines will have shown you that your story, as it stands, is unlikely that it will sell. The reason being that our protagonist is divorced. The People's Friend is a traditional magazine that values 'family'. Their guidelines require that readers:

"Like real material, but not realistic enough--with sex and violence, drink, etc.--that they are afraid or saddened. They believe in the sanctity, and the importance, of marriage.

The People's Friend can probably handle the divorce (if handled sensitively), but it cannot deal with the ex-husband's affair and the fact that he decided to throw him out.

There are two ways to approach this story if it is your idea. You could write it exactly as planned and target Woman's Weekly. Woman's Weekly will accept stories that explore the complications and implications associated with marital breakups. You won't be able to use the same themes as the magazine editors, so make sure to add something creative or reflective to your story.

The People's Friend could offer you another option: Rewrite your story. For this purpose, your protagonist could be a widow who has relied too heavily upon her husband in the past to help with the housework. If you create a story that shows her overcoming a problem on her terms, you can show her that she does have what it takes to keep going with her life.

It might be a good idea to show her looking forward at the challenge and how proud her husband would be of her accomplishments.

Do you see the difference between stories for these magazines? People's Friend would want a traditional, nostalgic and sentimental story. Woman's Weekly is looking for a new perspective on an old problem. It would also like to highlight the strength and independence that women today have.

This is just one example that illustrates the diversity of story markets. This book is not able to address all the nuances and subtleties in each magazine. Analyzing the markets that you are most interested is the best approach. If you've completed the writing exercise prior, you should already be able to identify the type of story you want. Look for at least three to four publications that feature this type of story. Compare them and try to understand the differences. This is when it becomes important to read magazines. You should not only read the stories but also analyze them.

Once you have selected three or four magazines to which you wish to submit your story, plan your next steps. The rest of the book will provide guidance on creating a great opening, structuring your plot and creating characters. Now, you can begin to identify some stories that would work well in the magazines you have chosen.

Write for these magazines. If you persist, you will see your stories accepted. Even if a story is rejected by a magazine you can request a revision to meet the requirements of another magazine. Do not just send it to another magazine. Rework it first. Then, adjust it to the needs and preferences of the next magazine editor.

Writing is a constant process. As you analyze markets and write more, your sixth sense will help you to predict what will work. You will instinctively know if a story is suitable for the magazine you want to target. If your gut feels that the story is not right, don't send them out.

Sometimes, even though you don't know a market for the story, you might get an idea that you want to write. Writing these stories takes time. Time you could have spent writing fiction you are confident selling. But, sometimes stories just need to be written.

If this happens, you will find other places for your work than the magazines markets. In the next chapter, we'll discuss this.

Chapter 5: Other ways you can get published

When you listen to my advice, you will always have a market in your mind when you write a story. You'll be able to determine how many words your story should contain and which approach you will need to succeed.

But--and it's always a BUT--what about those stories? The ones that just nag at you in your brain and beg to be written.

Do not ignore that feeling if it happens to you. You will find that the stories you are trying to suppress become louder and more insistent as you go along, until they overwhelm you. The only way to get rid of clutter in your head is to pay attention to the story that is nagging at you. Let it go. Write the story, and then see what happens. You might be lucky and your story could become the perfect magazine cover.

There are two other options available if the above is not possible.

You can start your search online for small press magazines and eZines, as well as websites that publish experimental short fiction or literary stories. These publishing platforms will often have guidelines you must follow but they are less rigid than those of magazines. There is one problem with these publishing options: they rarely pay for stories. And if they do, it's often a very small amount.

Publishing your work via these channels has its benefits. This means that your work is read, which many would argue is the main purpose of all authors. It allows you to add the story credit onto your writing CV. Thirdly, you can add the story credit to your writing CV. Readers who enjoy your stories may be interested in more. This could be useful if your next publication idea is...

Self-publishing of your stories as eBook collections. This is another method to publish stories that can't or won't be published in magazines. However, this does not mean that you should self-publish stories which aren't of high quality. Do your best work, especially if it's to gain a following.

You can also make an eBook out of stories you've published in the past. However, this is only possible if you still have the copyright. Usually, magazines buy the first rights for your work. All rights revert to the author once the story appears in the magazine. The second right to the story can be sold to another market if that happens. However, this is not usually possible as editors don't like work that's been published in other magazines. You could also wait until your stories are complete to self-publish them.

Another option is to submit non-standard stories to writing competitions. Remember that competition rules can be just as rigid, if not stricter than editor's requirements. A competition doesn't allow you to submit any type of story. A competition will typically have a word limit and a theme. The story must also be specific to the genre. If your story does not meet all these requirements, you should not enter the contest. Open competitions can be much more flexible. These competitions allow stories from many genres to be submitted.

Competitions: The drawbacks

You might be able to submit your story if there is a competition you are interested in. What do you have to lose?

You might have a lot to lose. Every competition usually has an entry cost. While the fees are used for prize money generation, they can also be quite expensive in certain cases. Given the low entry fee and the fact creative writing competitions often receive thousands (or hundreds) of entries, your chances of getting an investment return are very slim.

There will usually be only one prize, but you will have to compete with many other writers. While a competition may have dozens or more excellent stories than would be published under other circumstances, only one winner is possible.

Writers' competitions

Finding writing contests is simple. Search for "writing competitions" in Google and you will be flooded with options. There are many well-established contests that offer huge prizes. But the rule of thumb here is that the more the prize, then the higher the entry fee. These competitions attract a lot of entries so you'll have to compete with many other writers.

Writing magazines, like Writing Magazine, Writer's Forum and Mslexia, in the UK and The Writer and Writer's Digest, in the USA, are great resources for information about contests. These magazines also host regular competitions.

Also, make sure to check with your local libraries and writing clubs to see if they have any competitions in your area. These are less likely than others to require an entry fee. However, they will receive fewer submissions. This is great news for you because you have a better chance of winning.

Many new writers enjoy the discipline of contests. They enjoy being assigned a theme, genre or word count. It can give them the inspiration they need to create a story. Although winning isn't easy, these tips will help you improve your chances.

Competitions: Improve your chances

Writing competitions often receive a lot of entries. If you submit a story with a unique voice, the chances of winning are very slim. Judges will not only expect submissions to meet the entry requirements, but will also be looking at stories that are exceptional, memorable or simply outstanding. Here are six tips to increase your chances of winning.

1. Respect the rules

It may sound obvious to follow the rules of competition, but any writing judge will tell anyone that every competition has some entries that should be disqualified. You might find that a contest has stated that the writer's name should not be included on the manuscript. This is a common rule, and it is intended to prevent bias in the judges. You might also be restricted to writing in a certain area or state. In this case, an entry from someone not in the qualifying area may have been accepted.

No matter the reason, rules are there to be followed. It's important to pay the entry fee and not waste it. Do not lose your entry fee. Do yourself a favor, and ensure you carefully read through the rules before you begin to write. You can also use them as a checklist before you start writing.

Do not forget to submit your story by deadline.

2. Be consistent with the word count

Technically, I believe the word limit is one of competition rules (see 1 above). It is worth mentioning the importance of staying within the word limit. It's easy to overlook. Some writers believe that an additional ten or twenty words will not pose a problem. Some writers extend the word limit to over 100 words. It is a risky tactic that can lead to your story getting disqualified. Some competition judges allow some margin for error, while others require that the word count be strictly adhered to.

Sometimes, writers must adhere to a very strict word limit. This is why they need to edit their work objectively and eliminate unnecessary words. It is possible to improve almost all stories by doing some careful pruning. Samuel Johnson said it best: "Wherever you come across a passage which is particularly fine, strike them out." We'll be discussing editing in a subsequent chapter.

3. Register for the right competitions

Some competitions offer large prizes. Fish Publishing offers a first-place prize of EUR3,000 but charges an outrageous EUR20 for entry. As I stated earlier, the higher the prize fund the greater your chances of winning. If there were any chance of winning, then I would not spend EUR20 on a contest.

Start with smaller competitions to improve your chances of winning. Your chances of winning are greater if the prizes are smaller. You'll also be able to write a CV detailing your prize if you win.

Don't let me deter you from participating in the big competitions if this is what you really want. However, be aware that these contests have high levels of competition and you'll be up to many other writers (including professional).

4. Professionally present your work

This chapter will cover how to format and present your stories. One thing to keep in mind when judging competitions is that they will be reviewing many stories one-by-one. They do not need manuscripts that are difficult to read or written in too small fonts.

A minimum of 12 font should be used and page numbers added to your story. You can print your entry on high quality white paper if it is hardcopy. The goal is to make your entry easy to read and understand.

Times New Roman or Garamond are good fonts, as well as Arial and Tahoma. It is important to leave enough margin for each side. This will allow the judges enough space to make notes about what you have to say, if they feel it is necessary.

5. Your work should be proof checked

Your stories must be thoroughly proofread before they are submitted, regardless of whether it's for a competition or a magazine editor. Spelling and grammar mistakes can distract readers and damage credibility as writers.

We'll be discussing proofreading techniques in a subsequent chapter. One of the best methods to identify errors in writing is to either read your work aloud or have someone else read it (preferably someone who can understand the English language).

You shouldn't rely solely on your computer's spelling checker to find spelling errors. Spell checkers are useful but won't catch misspelled words such as "there" instead or "their", or "bare" instead than 'bear", etc.

Before you send it, make sure that your story is perfect, spelling included.

6. Make your theme work for you

If you are asked to submit a story for a competition that has a specific theme, it is often a good idea. This is because the first interpretation or idea you come up with is the most likely one to be accepted by others. Your stories should be memorable. Avoid familiar stories.

There will likely be many entries that share the same theme as the one being entered if there is a theme. A pile of stories with similar themes will be read by the judge. If your story can stand out among the pile, you'll be ahead of others.

Consider, for example, that you have been asked by a publisher to write a story on the retirement theme. Think about some storylines that might be possible. This is what I came to:

Irresistible (and obvious!) story idea: A person who is recently retired and is helping their spouse.

Second story idea: Someone who has retired but is financially stressed or bored. You could tell the story about how they found a new group to join or take up a hobby to earn an income.

It's a less obvious idea to tell a story about someone who is old but has retired. You could have a main character who is a retired professional football player or from the armed or police forces. The story and character could take you to new places.

A story that was written from the first idea would end up being a boring, repetitive tale.

Because the story has been written many times before, it is a cliche.

Combining the first idea with a clever twist and novel approach could work. However, your main character is likely an older person. Most of the characters in the competition stories will also be older.

A third, less obvious option could lead to something different. Imagine a professional footballer at 28 who is forced to retire because of injury. Your main character would stand out and be more memorable for judges. Your idea must be combined with a strong plot and well-written story. If you are able to do this, you will have a much better chance of creating a winning entry.

It doesn't matter what your theme is, you need to make it an integral part of your story. It's not possible to just pick up an old story and adapt it to fit the set theme. It is rarely a good idea just to shoehorn an existing story in a theme.

Don't lose heart

Even if your competition entry is exceptional, there is no guarantee that it will win. You shouldn't be too disappointed if it happens. Competitions will get a lot of entries. The fact that your story didn't win is not a sign of how great it is.

If your story isn't selected but you are confident in its merits as fiction, it might be possible to adapt it for publication. If your story is still worthy of publication, you should not submit it.

Assessment of your opportunities

Even though magazine markets can be tough, it is likely that you will have more success submitting your article to an editor than entering a competition.

If we stop and think about it, this puts us right back at the beginning: having a market in mind for your story before you begin to write. Are you feeling the same? You might recognize it as my mantra. Before we move on, however, I want me to stress once more how important it it to:

* Focus your writing on a particular market.

* Write in a way that appeals to the target audience.

* Match your word count to editor's requirements.

This is the best thing you can do to increase your chances at success as an author. Remember this.

Next we'll be looking at the elements of writing required to create a short tale. This is the exciting part. Prepare to write!

Chapter 6: Where do your ideas come from?

This is the common question writers receive. I have always answered this question when it comes up to me: Ideas are everywhere. This answer is often not satisfactory, frustrating or both for most aspiring writers. They don't fully understand the concept. They ask for more details. They want the magic equation.

There is no quick fix. Sometimes stories don't just pop out of a writer's head fully-formed. Although it does happen sometimes, it's not common.

A writer will likely see, hear, or read something that will spark an idea. It will start as a seed and, if nurtured, will eventually become a fully-formed story idea.

Think like you are a writer

If you are able to start writing and think like one, you will see that story ideas are all around you. There will be many ideas you find every day, in many places and in many different ways. You'll find that ideas come to you so often and in such a rapid pace that it will be difficult to remember how to put them down. Here are some ways I get ideas for short stories.

Your own experience is a great way to draw inspiration. Your writing will become authentic when you draw on your own past experiences. It will allow you to recall what you experienced and how it affected you, and you will be able express that emotion in your fiction.

Overheard bits of conversation: While I don't advocate that you become an omniscient observer, there are times when it is possible to listen in on conversations without their knowledge. It could be while you wait in line at the bank or train station or in a doctor's surgery. Or you may catch the strangest bits of conversation that someone is passing by.

I heard someone tell her friend, "Matthew always blames that on his dodgy legs." Naturally, I was curious. Blames it on what?

Matthew, you ask? It got me thinking and forming my own answers.

Save newspaper clippings from interesting and rare articles in magazines and newspapers.

It is also a good idea to save inspiring photos or images from magazines that you find interesting and worthwhile. These pictures could be of people or places or anything else that stimulates your imagination.

People watching is like listening to the conversations of others, but it takes a little more imagination. People watching is something I enjoy doing in a cafe or station. I watch people's body language, how they dress and what they carry. I then try and imagine the kind of person they might be, where they are now or what their past experiences have been.

TV programs and documentaries: These television programs, like newspaper and magazine articles can give you plenty of inspiration to write fiction. For inspiration, consider viewing the science and history channels.

Dreams: You may have dreams that give you story ideas. But, what may seem like a great plot in the middle the night can often become laughable or ridiculous in the cold light. You should always keep a notepad handy at your bed.

Titles: Find a great title, and then write a story. Although this sounds like putting the horse before it, it can work if your title is catchy and strong. Many of you may have heard something in the past, and thought, "Hey that would make a great title to a song...or for a story." Now, take the title down and write your story.

You can find inspiration in proverbs, quotations, and other sources. Themes can be useful because they help you structure your story and keep it focused.

CHARACTERS (roll twice)	TRAITS (roll twice)	SETTING (roll once)	PROBLEM (roll once)
Social worker	Boredom	Busy street	Feels betrayed
Retired nurse	Nervousness	Cabin in the woods	Lost purse/wallet
Six-year-old girl	Arrogance	Cinema/movie theater	Exam nerves
Celebrity chef	Vindictiveness	Book signing	Memory loss
Hotel receptionist	Disillusionment	School assembly hall	Hiding a secret
Politician	Fear	Beach	Mistaken identity

Ask "What is it if?": Use a character to start your questioning. Why are they doing this? What is their motivation? What motivates them? What are their secrets? What do these people do for a living and what do they do? What kind house do they live? What if things aren't what they seem? For drama or intrigue, think outside the box.

Listen to other stories. Market research should include this. While you are reading, consider whether you would write the story this way. Would you have altered the motivations of your characters? How would

CHARACTERS (roll twice)	TRAITS (roll twice)	SETTING (roll once)	PROBLEM (roll once)
English teacher	Anger	English village	Food allergy
Conservationist	Untrustworthiness	Hospital	Seeking revenge
Fashion model	Roger	Roadside café/diner	Adultery
80-year-old woman	Vanity	Grocery store	A crime
Wedding planner	Spitefulness	Car boot/garage sale	Loneliness
Police Officer	Drunkenness	Antique shop	Misguided loyalty

your ending differ from the one in story? What would you do to alter the setting? Before you know what, you might have a completely new idea to create a piece fictional of your own.

Mind mapping: Mind mapping allows you to tap into your creative side. Place a word at the center of a piece o paper and follow it. Create a map using balloons, lines, boxes, and arrows.

List the things you are most familiar with the central word. When you are done, consider using some of the words and ideas to create a new story.

Myths of legends and fairy stories: Create a contemporary story that is based upon a myth, legend, or fairy tale. This story could be modernized versions of Little Red Riding Hood stories, Cinderella stories, or a quest story that has the characters searching for the Holy Grail.

CHARACTERS (roll once)	TRAITS (roll once)	SETTING (roll once)	PROBLEM (roll once)
Factory worker	Impatience	A ranch or farm	Low self-esteem
Dentist	Uncertainty	Shopping centre/mall	Poor sense of direction
New mother	Unhappiness	Isolated old house	Phobia
Famous author	Confidence	Cruise ship	No money
Recluse	Tiredness	Remote island	Running late
Entrepreneur	Scepticism	Motorway highway	A broken promise

Photographs, objects and images: Sometimes strong images, objects, or characters can be used as the basis for a story. It could be an extravagantly designed hat, a gorgeous piece of jewelry, or a painting that you have seen in a museum. Maybe you're just walking through the park to see an elderly lady sitting on a park bench laughing. Who is she exactly? Is she really laughing?

While walking my dog one day, I got a chance to tell a story. As we were walking along a road, my dog stopped and took a quick look. She loves sniffing. I was walking along a road when my dog stopped to sniff the air. It was a door that looked similar to the British semi-detached homes built in the 1930s. You might be wondering "So what?". The truth is, the door was installed to a block containing flats that were built in 1973. It looked strange.

Why did it exist? Once I'd asked the one question, "Why", I started making up my own answers. Soon, I had an idea of a story. This story was written and sold to The People's Friend. It was a gentle story about a lady who, as she ages, decides that her beloved house, which holds so many memories for herself, is no longer necessary and moves to a smaller house. This isn't a sad tale about someone's end. It's positive and uplifting. We can take our memories with us wherever we go. For good measure, the woman's family made arrangements for her old front doors, which she considered to have a special meaning to her, to be fitted at her house in order to help her settle in to her new home.

Ask "Why?": The example above shows that asking why is a great method to generate a unique and original idea for your short story. Why did this person do that? Why did they say it? Why are they doing this? Why are they acting this way? Why? Why? Why? Do not take everything at face value when you create your story idea. Writers don't stop at the obvious. Make use of your imagination. Allow your imagination to run wild. It will take you to a story that people will enjoy.

There are many other methods to generate story ideas. You can even download an app to do it, as you might imagine. A+ Writing Tips by writing.com is the one that I have. It gives prompts that can be based on news or sketches, as well as scenes or words. You can also use it in multiple ways to get ideas for your story. It's very affordable and useful for anyone who is on the move but doesn't have access or time to keep a notebook or clippings.

There are many websites and books that provide prompts for writing stories.

Write down your ideas

It is a good habit to notate story ideas when you think of them. Ideas can be very sneaky and slippery. It is easy to forget about ideas if you don't take the time to write them down. I don't know how many times that I've had an awesome idea and then realized that it was gone. It's frustrating. To solve this problem, I now keep a journal in which I record my thoughts. I also use my smartphone to get an idea when my notebook is gone.

Creative writing exercises

It is not possible to wait for the inspiration to strike as a writer. A creative writing exercise can help you get your imagination going if it's difficult to find new ideas from the people and things around you. Many websites provide prompts for writing, story titles and ideas generators. You can simply Google "creativewriting exercises" to find out more.

Sometimes, it can be helpful to be told about what to write about. It can spark our creativity. These Cook-Ups-a-Story pages give you some ingredients to create a story. The amount of each ingredient that you use and the way you combine them is entirely up to your discretion. There are three tables that you can choose from.

All columns are numbered between 1 and 6. Roll the dice twice to choose two ingredients from each column. For example, if numbers 2 and 4 are rolled in the first table, your main characters in your short story would be a retired nursing professional and a celebrity chef. If you roll the same numbers twice (let's just say number 4,) you can write a story about 2 (or possibly more) celebrity chefs. Or, you could roll a 3rd time to get a new number.

For the first two columns (characters, traits and setting), roll the dice twice. To create a fantastic story, combine your ingredients.

Try it and see what results you get.

Chapter 7: Making a great introduction

This section will explain why it is crucial to create a compelling opening for your story. It's essential, I can assure you.

When you are writing a novel, the freedom to use entire pages or entire chapters is yours. The situation is different for short fiction. Writing a short story is different. You need to hook the reader from the very beginning.

Also, audience does not just refer to your readers. Your story will also be sent to the editor of the magazine. He or she will decide whether the story is worth publishing, and if it merits a readership.

Remember that magazines receive hundreds, if not thousands, of unsolicited manuscripts each week. These are the people that decide whether to buy stories. So you will need to get them to read your story and grab their attention right away. They will stop reading if this doesn't happen. Your story will not be accepted.

You should also look at the openings in the magazines you want to target as part of your market analysis. Do they always start with dialogue or action? Are most stories based on action or drama?

A good opening should achieve at least one. They:

* Write a question for the reader.

* Start at the moment of change in the main character's life.

* Introduce a type of problem.

* Are captivating enough to make you want to continue reading.

It is important to make an impact on your story opening. There are many ways that you can do this.

Action: Place the reader in the center of the action. This will get them excited to keep reading for the next part. Here are some examples.

I was in the garden hanging laundry when I smelled smoke. My first fear was for my newly laundered sheets. I then turned to see flames flickering in an upstairs windows of my home.

This is an example for a dramatic scene. The protagonist is in the backyard watching the unfolding drama. Is anyone inside the house? Is there anyone in the house? What's the next step?

Katy, six, raced towards the house with her head down and pumping her elbows.

These two words are key: 'Six-year-old' & 'Sanctuary'. What did the child fear and run for safety?

It's important to start conversations: Many stories open with interesting or revealing dialogue. Here's one example.

It is appropriate for stories targeted at younger readers

Aunt Agnes stated, "You have disobeyed me child."

Who is the child, and why? And who's Aunt Agnes and what is their relationship? This shows that the child is in serious trouble. What happens next? Or will the child be punished for their actions? Or, will he/she be able speak their mind out of the trouble? And what have they done?

Sound effects: Bring readers right into the action with sounds. You can take this as an example:

Helen stormed out of the house and Bang left the door. It was not again, I thought. There was no more row. I waited for Gran's bones china to stop rattle, and then, slowly, I opened the front door and began my search for Helen.

This is a story about a family drama. "Another round" indicates a dysfunctional relationship. Who is Helen and who are the protagonists? And why are they there at his/her grandmother's? Will there be a reconciliation? Or will it escalate into something worse than this?

The night was darkened by the sound of the siren. I knew I was done when I heard the siren's mocking and insistent wail.

This is an indication that a crime has occurred or is about to occur. Are you hearing the sirens of a police vehicle? Or an ambulance. Who are they and what do they do? What happens next

Character: Start by giving a description of a fascinating and unusual character. You could use this example:

Charlie Munrow's left eyelobe had been bit in a fight. He was seated in the emergency department of the hospital, pressing a moist towel against his ear.

This is quite a shocking scene. It's quite vicious when someone's ear is bit off. Charlie Munrow, who is he and why did he fight?

Who was he fighting and why? And where will this story end?

As you can see, a great opening raises questions in your mind. What happens next? What is the identity of this person? Why are they in this situation. These questions will drive people to read more. These people will be searching for answers, so ensure that your story provides them with those answers.

If your opening story has something that is interesting, intrigues, puzzles or even shocks the reader, you're on the right track. Start with action, dialogue and sound effects. You can also include interesting characters or any combination of these things. Your story opening should include at least some of the following five Ws: Who.

Don't overwhelm the reader with too much information in the beginning of your story. Too much information can cause confusion and make the story difficult to understand.

Your story opening will be your 'shop windows'. You can draw readers in to the story with the right touches.

Your story will not be accepted if it has a good opening. However, well-crafted characters and a strong structure are essential to a successful ending. An opening paragraph is the most important part of a story. Without it, nobody will read beyond that first paragraph. Your story will be lost if the opening is weak.

My job as a teacher and writer of creative writing means that I often have to read short stories from new writers. Opens that are too long, rambling, or otherwise irrelevant are two things I am often faced with. A lot of beginners think they have to set the stage before the action can begin. This is false. You should place the story right in the middle. We don't need line upon line of descriptions of the setting, character attire, and weather (which seems like a popular choice for new writers).

I often read through a story written from a beginner, and after three or four paragraphs, find the beginning of the story. This is a question you should ask yourself about the opening of a piece.

* Does it happen in the middle action or drama?

* If the dialogue begins with an opening, does it reveal anything significant or unexpected?

* Is there any sense of intrigue, shock or conflict in the story opening? If so, does it make you want more?

If you are unable to answer at least one of these questions then you should reconsider how you started your story. Keep reading to the next, third, and fourth paragraphs. Is this really where the action begins? You could also start the story there.

The tone or mood of the story should be set in the opening. This is how you let your readers know the story will be. You should give a hint if you're writing horror stories.

Even if it's a subtle hint. A crime story should have some criminal intent or action in the opening paragraphs. A story about family relationships that introduces the characters and hints at the problem/conflict they are experiencing should be short.

Warning: When opening stories, be careful

There's a chance that you will try to perfect your opening paragraph but never get on with writing the rest. Do not let this happen. You shouldn't allow your opening lines to get in the way.

Try to do the best that you can. However, once you've written the story, you can always edit it. In fact, the whole story will need editing, so don't let poor writing stop you. Keep writing. Moving on to the middle and ending of your story.

Chapter 8: Structures and plot

Here's a question for you? Do you believe structure and plot are one thing? Are structure and plot the same thing?

Personally, I believe structure and plot are story elements that are inextricably connected. This is why I decided to combine them in this chapter.

Let's begin by discussing the differences.

What is plot?

If it's a good story, the plot is what keeps readers reading. It's the thing that keeps you turning to the next page. Sometimes novels are called 'page-turners' or fast-paced'. This is due to their effectiveness.

Each story, regardless of whether it's a novella or a short piece of fiction, is made up of a series (or a collection of) of events. These events are called the plot. It's the story's order. Many of the events that occur in your story are a continuation of an event that occurred earlier or as a result or a conflict that your main character is facing. A story's plot will grow in complexity over time. It will build up to a point of climax or a moment of change. When the story reaches its conclusion, or when all the problems have been solved, the plot is complete. This is often referred to by the term "story resolution" (or "denouement")

If we were asked to plot a novel's plot lines, we would most likely find that they are a series of ups-and-downs that build to the climax and then fade away at the end.

The plot of a short story tends to be simpler because you have less time and less words. The plot does not consist of many ups and falls. It builds steadily to the story's climax, or resolution, then drops sharply. When a short story's main problem or conflict has been resolved, it is time to end. More details will be provided in a subsequent chapter.

You can see the diagram at chapter's end. It illustrates the basic plot structure of a short story. This diagram can be copied and kept on your writing desk to remind you of the structure of your story.

What is a plot?

A plot is not just a sequence of events. Let's consider Kevin, a fictional character. Kevin rises each morning, has breakfast, showers, and then heads off to work. This is a sequence of events. It is not a plot.

Imagine Kevin getting up one morning, and hearing the doorbell. It's the courier with a parcel. Kevin's pet dog escapes after he signs to receive the package. Kevin now has an issue. If he runs off to find the dog, he will be late to work. He also has an important meeting that morning. Kevin must be present to discuss a possible promotion. If he isn't, he can say goodbye to the promotion. Kevin is looking for that promotion since his wife left him recently and he's having trouble paying his mortgage. Kevin cannot just leave his dog on the streets and go to work. Kevin loves his dog. Kevin usually walks his dog during lunch, but can't leave it outside until then. Anything could happen...

I won't go on because, let's be honest, I don't know what this story is about! Can you see what i mean? There are many events in this series, but also many problems. Some problems have an impact on others.

What is structure?

It's always difficult for me to determine the plot without structure. It's all about the form or design of the story. Your structure is what you use for putting the story together.

The simplest structure possible is that a tale has a beginning. A middle. And an end. However, how could your story be structured differently? Maybe it could be a circle structure. The story begins at a time of crisis or excitement, and then it uses flashback to show how the character got there. We'll get into flashback more in the next chapter. The story then returns to the present, and finally the resolution. To give the story a satisfying feeling of completeness and resolution, you can use a circular structure that links the beginning to the end.

Another option is to arrange your story around two viewpoints. A novel will usually have each chapter assigned to one viewpoint. If you are writing a short story, it is necessary to break it into sections. Each section should be told from the point of view of a character. The best way to limit the number characters in a story is to keep it to two. With a shorter story, you may be able to manage three perspectives but no more. This type of story shows conflicting perspectives and allows for different views to be presented on a problem. This story presents both sides of a story.

It is possible to create a story using a combination of emails, letters, postcards, diary entries and newspaper articles. These are epistolary stories. Some of the best-known novels using this format are 84 Charing Cross Road (Helene Hanff), The Screwtape Letters (C S Lewis), Bridget Jones's Diary (Bridget Jones), and the Adrian Mole Series by Sue Townsend.

To summarize, structure is the way a story is organized or designed. A good structure will help to bring balance or symmetry into a story.

How can you create a structure or plot of land?

Answering this question depends on how good you are at writing. Planning your story before you start writing is the best and smartest way. You can make a list of the following things in advance.

* characters

* This is the beginning point for your story

* Possible scenes

* The main storyline

* The ending.

It doesn't have to be very detailed. A rough outline is enough to get your mind organized so you can start writing.

Here's a template I included at the end of this chapter that you can use as a guide to creating an outline for your stories. It's based on the conventional plot structure and has a few prompts for you.

This is a method I do not use all the time, if truth be told. It could be that I haven't felt the need to write anything down in years of writing. However, before I start writing, my story outline is always in my head. Once I have an idea, I let it develop in my brain for many weeks. I then start writing once I'm certain I understand where it's heading. I will usually write the story I want, nine times out of ten. But every now and then, a new (often more satisfying) ending comes to me while I write. I insert the new ending into the story and close it when that happens.

If you're new at writing and believe you need a structure or organisation to help you organize your thoughts, I strongly suggest that you draw out your story first on paper before you start writing. You might be able to outline your story more easily in your head than you did on paper as you learn and improve your writing technique. You don't want your time to be wasted, so it's worth knowing where your story is going before you start.

No matter what way you choose to organize your stories and how they are laid out, it is worth starting to plan a story that you'd like to write.

Short story template

Asking yourself these questions can help you

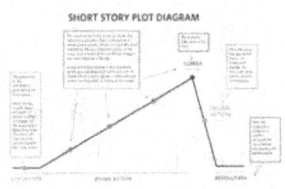

to create a story overview. This plan will be helpful as you draft your first draft.

Story title

Is there a common theme in your story? If so, what theme is it?

What is your main character's goal? What are their goals?

What is your main character's motivation? WHY are they determined to achieve their goal

What kind of problem (conflicts) will your main character encounter that will keep them from achieving the goal?

Your story opens in HOW, WHEN, or WHERE? Does your story open with action or dialogue? Or a moment in crisis or change?

What is the first time your main character meets a conflict or a problem?

How does your main character react to this problem What do they do?

What is the 2nd point of conflict? This could arise from the actions of your character or the natural consequences of the first.

What is your main character's response to the second issue?

What is the principal crisis point (the CLIMAX or the story's core)? This is your character's most important or worst moment.

How would you react in this situation of crisis? What character traits do they show in their response? Is your story finished?

Your story should end with your main character solving the problem. You should tie your resolution to something your main characters did or said earlier. Do not rely on any outside forces or chance to solve the problem. You will disappoint your reader if this happens.

Consider whether the main character of your story has made any changes or learned something along the way.

Chapter 9: Using flashbacks

When you write a novel, it is possible to create stories that span years, decades, or even your entire life. The action of a short story tends to be shorter. It can take place for just a few hours or even a day. Some stories are short and focus on a brief interaction between two characters.

Short stories are characterized by an immediate feeling. They can be compared to short videos which record key moments or dramatic scenes.

Successive short stories, even those that are the shortest, will often reference the past in some fashion or provide backstory. This happens when characters think about the past in relation to what is happening now.

This is flashback. This allows writers to include relevant information about events that took place before the story began. Your characters may reflect upon events that took place years, or even centuries ago. Real life is like that. Our minds wander all around the place.

It will be a reminder of something past or a way to remember the events in my life that have shaped who I am today.

Past events often influence our motivations and can even drive them. The past influences our behaviour and how we respond to situations.

Flashback can play an important role in your story. This will enable you to provide important background information and help develop character. Sometimes it is the past that makes your characters hesitate about doing certain things and moving their lives in the right direction.

In my chapter about story openings, I suggested you start your story at the beginning of the story. This is where the main character will be experiencing drama or change. For story writers, it is a good idea to open a story at the beginning of an action. You will likely have to use flashback to show what the characters did to reach that crisis point.

Flashback drawbacks

Flashbacks can lead to readers losing the core of the story if they go off-topic too often. You might start with two people meeting at a restaurant. Then you launch into long flashbacks, which can lead readers to forget that the main characters are there. It will be a pleasant surprise when you do eventually come back to them.

Rule number one: Avoid flashbacks. If you are required to give a lot of backstory, only do so in small chunks. Recall the present time often to remind your readers where and how the story is set.

Rule number two: You should only use flashbacks to refer back to past events that relate to what's happening right now. You don't want your characters to be reminiscing about people or events that have no relevance to the plot.

Rule number three: Give clear signals to your readers that the story is falling into flashback.

Let's say we create a story about Mark (Laura) and Laura (Laura). We would use this signal to have Laura slip into flashback.

Laura recalled when Mark and she first shared a meal together. It was Mark's home. He'd prepared them pasta and joked about playing the role as flamboyant server.

He had asked Madamoiselle if he would like to taste the wine.

Laura had laughed and sipped on the wine before she nodded her approval. She was not able to tell the difference between quality wine and low-quality plonk. Although it all tasted identical to her, she was unwilling to reveal that to Mark. He was smart and highly educated about these subjects, and she did not want him to believe that she was a philistine.

You will see in this example that I used the recalled trigger to show that Laura is reflecting back on past events. We then used pluperfect for a while. He'd made them pasta and, jokingly he played the role of flamboyant server. Pluperfect can be translated as a tense used to indicate an action that has taken place in the past. For instance, he/she had/it had.

It's obvious that we've removed the pluperfect tense in the last line of paragraph 2. The flashback scene is now as if it were happening now.

Read the next chapter to see how flashback works in real life. It's called Gently Does It. It is a relationship story that was sold to one of the women's magazines. The flashback technique is used at many points.

As you read it, you'll find that I have made comments and taken notes at the flashback points. I hope that this helps you to see how flashback can help you insert back story into your own fiction.

Chapter 10: Gently Does It

Joanne watched as Lily prodded relentlessly at the pineapple and Ham pizza slice.

Alice said, matter-of-factly: "Lily doesn't eat pizza." "I thought I knew that."

Lily explained that she likes the pineapple and ham, as well as the base. It's the cheddar I don't like."

Joanne patted Lily in the hand. "It doesn't matter. "Eat the pineapple and ham. Leave the cheese out."

"But it's all melted. It sticks to everything. Even the pineapple.

"Could I make you sandwiches instead?"

Six-yearold Lily nodded. "I'm sorry, Joanne."

"It's all fine, sweetie. It's your fault. I should have inquired. I thought all children enjoyed pizza."

Joanne also made another mistake when she butter thin slices of bread. Sometimes, being a stepmother was not an easy role to play.

This story opens in a moment when Joanne is facing a crisis. However, it is not a major one. Joanne has a problem with pizza. Although it's not life-threatening, her dislike of pizza is indicative. Alice, Alice's stepmother, has assumed her role and is finding it hard to connect with her daughters. We first fall into flashback at this stage (see below).

It was all so fresh to her. It had been seven months since Will first met her at the New Year's Eve party of a mutual buddy.

Joanne had been taken by the hand of his host just before midnight and led into his garden. He initially said that he wanted to avoid the push-and-pull of "Auld Lang Syne," but later, he admitted that it was just an excuse for Joanne to go her way.

Outside, he had removed his jacket, wrapped it around Joanne's shoulders, and walked outside in the freezing winter garden. They had gazed at stars and watched the fireworks explode in frenzied blasts of green-purple.

Joanne states that it has been seven months since Joanne met Will ...'. This signals to the reader she is recalling past events. After a while, we shift to the pluperfect tense...

In fact, pluperfect tense will be used for the first three paragraphs in this flashback (up until the point at which the fireworks explode with furious blasts green and purple). The pluperfect tone is dropped and the story continues as flashback (see below).

Joanne was invited to dinner by Will, who told her that he was now a widower with two children.

Will was destined to be your partner. It was irreversible.

Joanne was well aware of how difficult it could be to form a relationship Will's girls.

He took her several weeks to introduce her to the girls. Their first meeting wasn't a huge success. Alice and Lily, who were shy and quiet, looked at Joanne from behind their long lashes.

Lily was Lily's youngest friend and she was also the most eager to make new friends. Will suggested they take a walk through the park. Lily reached out to Joanne and followed her.

Alice was eight years of age and much more detached. She was eighteen and seemed more aloof than usual. She had followed her, kicking on the asphalt.

Joanne and the girls were left alone when Will called from his customer after they had returned to the house.

Alice looked at Joanne's short, red-colored hair and declared "Mummy had blonde hair." "It was long wavy. It was like liquid gold," Daddy used remark.

Joanne said "That sounds beautiful." "I'm sure that she was very beautiful," Joanne said.

"She was. Would you like to view some photos?"

Joanne, overcome by curiosity, allowed Alice and Lily into the dining room. Alice took out an antique box from underneath the sideboard and chose a group of photographs to spread over the table.

They looked through the snaps for ten more minutes, laughing at Will and Alice's school pictures and giggling as they took baby photos of Lily. Helen, Will's wife was photographed, and it was certainly stunning.

Will found them together, sitting around the table looking at Helen's photographs.

Alice stated to Joanne that she wanted to see photos of Mummy.

"I didn't... I..." Joanne felt silly. In fact, it was her daughter's idea. She was too close to Alice and Lily, the trust she had established in them over the last few minutes, to abandon her loyalty. Instead she shrugged.

Joanne wondered whether Will was shocked at her behavior. She smiled at him and knew that everything would be alright.

Alice continued, "I was telling Alice she was so beautiful Mummy." "She was beautiful. She wasn't, Daddy?"

"Yes, she was."

"The most beautiful woman anywhere in the world. Ever. Is that not right?

Will picked up Helen's photo and took on a look of uncertainty.

He responded, "I used believe so," "Now I don't think so."

Alice demanded "What do YOU mean?"

"Well, Lily is just like her mother. Perhaps even prettier. I think you two might be the most beautiful women in all of humanity. Ever."

Joanne smiled, astonished at Will's sensitiveness.

Will kissed his girls later, after the girls had tucked themselves into bed.

"You know what? I think that you are beautiful. These things I've said earlier... it's ..."

"Don't worry Will. There's no need to explain. I understand."

He said, "I'm glad your do," adding that he didn't think he could understand him.

Will proposed as such.

To signal that flashback is finished, the last sentence of the above section slips back into pluperfect. Now, the story is moving forward in time. However, flashback continues. To indicate that a time period has passed, a line of dots should be used. The passage of time should be indicated in your manuscript with an additional space. If desired, you may also add a line of asterisks. This is a great tool to use to move a story forward. It's a quick story equivalent to a new page.

Here we use the pluperfect ('The Wedding HAD been wonderful. This is a reminder that these are events from the past. After three paragraphs, again the pluperfect is dropped.

*****

The wedding was wonderful. Alice and Lily were wonderful bridesmaids at the elegant riverside ceremony.

The honeymoon was actually more of a family holiday. Joanne and Will resisted the temptation to leave their children for 2 weeks. Instead, they decided to go on a family holiday to Crete. This would allow them to get to really know one another.

Joanne returned from the beach looking tanned, relaxed, and she had settled into a regular routine to manage her new job as stepmother while still working as a recruitment consultant.

They managed to keep their heads together admirably, all things being equal. They were always a bit nervous about eating.

Will did his fair share of the cooking but was not a great chef. Joanne, who had no time to cook complex meals, did her best, even if this meant she used a few jars of cook-in sauces.

On a hot sunny day, approximately a month following their return from Crete they decided to prepare a cold buffet with honeyed Ham, cherry tomatoes, celery sticks new potatoes and chunks of buttery bread. She took out a jar with pickled beetroot to add to her dish.

Alice said that her mother used to buy fresh beetroot, boil it and then cook it. "It was tedious, but it was worthwhile. Her beetroot turned out to be absolutely delicious.

Joanne ignored the comments and asked the girls if they were ready to eat.

It's a boiled beetroot. Joanne said it was in the same class as home-made jams or pickles. All fine and dandy if time allowed. Supermarket beetroot was, for Alice, perfectly acceptable and much more convenient. Alice's remarks had hurt.

Here the story returns back to the present. It actually returns the story to a point a few more days from where it began. The opening lines of the story point out this fact to the reader. "So, a few more days after the ham & pineapple pizza blunder ...').

This is the end of flashbacks and the narrative continues forward.

Joanne decided to try again a few days later after the pineapple pizza and ham blunder.

It was the summer holidays so she took a few days off. Will managed his business from his home, while he was busy writing a tender for a crucial contract. Joanne offered to look after his girls while he was preparing the tender details.

Joanne had bought a piece ham to roast and fresh beetroots to boil to please Alice. After she had put her ham joint in the oven with the beetroot, she went back to check on the girls.

She discovered them reading quietly in their living room. Joanne knew Will was at work in his office back at the house.

Joanne suggested, "Shall we play games?"

Alice put down the book. "What kinda game?"

Joanne said, "How about Scrabble?" Joanne desperately tried to recall the handful of board games in the cupboard below the stairs.

Alice groaned. "Bor-ing. "Bor-ing.

Lily suggested that "we could watch a Disney film."

"Even more boring," Alice said. "I've seen all of them at least a thousand different times."

"How about Monopoly?"

"Monop what?"

Joanne repeated the phrase "Monopoly". "Have ye ever played it?"

Joanne and Joanne both sighed, realizing that they had found something to keep them entertained for a while.

She went into the kitchen, checked the hams and the beetroots, then pulled out the Monopoly card from under the stairs.

She said, as she stepped into the living area, "Right," and asked, "What do your fancy?" The iron or the battleship, the boot, the iron, a top hat or dog?

Joanne had lost track of the time-consuming game Monopoly, especially when she was teaching beginners, especially younger ones. After clarifying the rules of purchasing houses and hotels and explaining the advantages of Mayfair Park Lane and Mayfair, Joanne was able to see how much fun she was having. Finally, she found something they all could enjoy for the first time in weeks.

Joanne was studying the chance card. Do not go. Do not collect PS200...

Lily asked "What's this funny smell?"

Joanne was on the floor in seconds. She ran to the kitchen, where she smelled incinerated meat and burnt beetroot. The girls followed her and snorted in disgust, pinching their noses.

Lily replied, "Yuk!"

Alice stated unnecessarily: "You've been burning the beetroot."

Lily said that she thought you had also smoked the ham.

Joanne donned an oven mitt and attempted to retrieve the charcoal-coloured pork.

Will noticed that the pungent smells had reached Will's office. He walked into his kitchen to investigate.

"Hasn't anyone ever said to you that you should boil beetroot?" he laughed. "Not fry."

Joanne took the oven mitt out of her hand and tossed it onto the kitchen worktop.

"I'll tell your what, why don't we get the tea?"

She then stomped out, her face as red and irritated as the beetroot they had just boiled.

Here, another break was used to indicate a slight shift in time. This is not a flashback since we are moving the narrative forward continually. But, notice that the opening line of this section gives the reader a clear indication to move the story forward to later that afternoon ('The girls were in their bed by eight-thirty the evening.').

The pluperfect is only briefly used in this section ("Lily HAD kissed Joanne goodbye") so you could say there is a flashback.

The story continues chronologically, until its conclusion.

*****

The girls were already in bed by 8:30 that evening. Joanne and Lily were both in bed by 8:30 that evening.

Joanne, we are grateful that you showed us how to play Monopoly. Do you think we can have another go tomorrow?

"Yes, sweetie. If you would like.

Joanne was able to recall how much Joanne and her husband had been enjoying themselves before they became a culinary disaster.

Will said to Will, after the girls had gone down to bed. "Too busy showing them how to cheat at Monopoly.

Joanne said, "We girls do not cheat."

Will laughed, and he swept her into the arms of his.

They were cuddled on the settee watching the last minutes of a quiz and then suddenly, their power supply went off. The electric fire,

TV, and television went dark, then they heard a sharp squeal coming from their bedroom.

Joanne was just behind Will as Will raced the stairs. Alice and Lily were lying in bed. Lily was grumbling and clutching her one-eyed bear.

She sniffed. "I'm frightened."

"Oh, do stop crying, Lily," Alice said. "You are such a baby. It's a short power cut.

Will sat down on his bed and pulled Lily to his knees.

He stroked her head, and said, "It is OK." "Daddy's Here... Joanne, Too."

The street lights were gone, and the bedroom was now darkened from the power blackout. Despite the absence electric light outside, there was a strong glow.

Lily pointed to the spot on her curtains where the glow was strongest and said, "There is a ghost outside." "Look!"

Joanne said that she believes it was the man in the moon who is shining his torch.

Alice laughed. "There's no such thing."

Joanne said, "And there is no such thing ghosts either," and threw the curtains open to reveal the pale, fat face of the moon staring in through the window. "Look, Lily. It's just the Moon. That's all."

Will asked Lily as he lay down and tucked Lily back into his bed.

"Alice said that ghosts appear at night in order to frighten people, particularly little girls."

Will said, "I think Alice is pulling your leg," and Alice looked frustrated. "It was very uncouth of her."

Lily asked Mummy, her voice almost whispering.

Joanne realized that Alice didn't want to know the answer from just Lily, judging by the intense look she saw on Alice's face.

Will held Lily's hand. "No, love. Mummy doesn't exist." She's in heaven."

Joanne turned Lily's head. "Are ye my mummy now?"

They all stopped talking, waiting for Joanne's reply.

Joanne paused to think about how what she said might impact their future. Then, she smiled.

"No, Lily. There will be only one mummy. But I promise, I'll always be your friend.

"I'll help Alice, and you, with the things that mothers do for their children. I will take good care and do my best for your welfare. Boiling beetroot is one thing that I cannot promise to do. It seems that I'm not very good at boiling beetroot.

Alice cracked a smile and Lily giggled.

That was the moment when the lights were turned on again and the nightlight started to glow.

Will declared, "There we have it," "everything's back on track." Now, get down and snuggle, you two. And, go to sleep.

"Goodnight, girls," said Joanne. "Sleep tight."

Alice called Joanne. "About Beetroot... it doesn't really matter, I know. The pickled version is very good to me.

"So do I." Joanne winked. "So do I."

I realize that this story is violating one of the rules I mentioned in my last chapter - the rule about not spending too much time in flashback. Gently Does It spends too much time reflecting upon past events. It works because once the flashback has begun, the story chronologically moves forward until it returns to the current time (a few weeks after the hamburger and pineapple pizza mishap that opened the story).

It is important to not confuse the reader with flashback. When you're done writing a story, take it apart and evaluate whether your flashbacks work. Are you clear? Do you have any signals to the reader that this story is about to enter a flashback situation?

Flashback is a story-writing technique that can be improved upon. If your first attempts are unsuccessful, don't despair.

Viewpoint

Writing fiction requires you to take into account your point of view. The question is, "Whose story is it?"

Short stories are easy: your main character will often be the one who tells the story. Sometimes it can be difficult to determine who the main characters are.

If you get an idea to tell a story, it is usually pretty clear who it should be told from. But, if your story involves strong personalities who are equally involved with the action, it may lead to them competing for the role as protagonist. If that happens, then you'll have to make a choice.

It is best to avoid making that choice. Avoiding making that decision could lead to a head-hopping story where you jump from one perspective to another. Here's how I mean it... and this is an example for how NOT you should do it.

George watched Anthony dribble towards him with his ball. He was enjoying himself again. It was typical Anthony! He was typical Anthony! He was frequently tackled well before he made it to the goal.

George shouted, "Over here!" Anthony must have seen that he was in better position to shoot. Why wasn't he giving the ball to him?

Anthony continued on his way to the goal, determined for a score. He thought: "I have to get one past the goalkeeper today." He knew he would be fired if he didn't.

He was at the goal mouth now. He looked down at the ground, then at the back, and took his shot.

George watched as Anthony's ball skimmed the goal post. He was stunned that Anthony had missed this one. It was a sitter.

Phew! What's the matter? This is just a brief example of what I mean by "head-hopping", but it will demonstrate my point. One minute, we're looking at Anthony in his head and the next, George is watching the ball fly through George's eyes.

If you were to tell this type of story, then you'd need to decide whether it should be told from George's point of view or Anthony's. After that, you would have the responsibility to only write it from that perspective.

Multiple perspectives

There is an alternative. This was something I spoke about in an earlier chapter as I talked about structure. The soccer story could be written in two perspectives--Anthony's and George's. But to do this you'd need to divide the story into sections. Each section would have only one point of view.

This story would be a good fit for this approach. The rivalry between George, Anthony and the other team could be shown by sharing the viewpoints and motivations of each character.

It is important to keep each viewpoint to a section of your story. Avoid mixing things up too much.

Viewpoint as a way for a story to be turned on its head

Sometimes, I will get an idea for the story and begin to write it down in my head. But then, I realize that it isn't working. This is usually because the story is too predictable or has been done many times before. For it to work, you need a new twist and a different approach.

You might consider changing the perspective of the story to get the new angle you want. While it might not work every time, it is worth a try. Let's say, for example, that two people meet up in a job interview situation. One person is the interviewee and the other the interviewer. The traditional approach to writing a story is to do it from the perspective the person being interviewed. By doing this, you can convey their nervousness, uncertainty, confidence loss, fears, hopes, and other emotions. It's a tedious, predictable path that can lead you to a boring or predictable story.

What if you wrote your story from the viewpoint of the interviewer instead? Maybe they're feeling nervous, or maybe they are new to the interview process. They might recognize the interviewee because they know them from their past. What will that say about whether they decide to offer the job? Will they be able to take revenge on the person or do they need to return a favor?

If you were to write the story from the perspective the interviewer, it would be a totally different story than the first.

Do you want to be the first or the third person?

While you are probably aware of the difference between third person and first-person viewpoints, I will remind you by using an opening taken from a short story I wrote years ago. It's written first person.

It was the most wonderful moment of all my life. I felt my soul emerge from the blackness and darkness of oblivion, freed from death's cold clutches.

I struggled slowly to get back to living, trying to remember who and what I had been through.

My eyes opened and I saw.

As you can see, the first person view is written so that the main character speaks directly to the reader. This was the greatest moment in my life...I felt myself emerge.

This approach has some advantages. This is a good approach if you are telling a story about something that happened to one person. It allows the main character to share his or her inner thoughts with the reader. It is a great way to characterize your story, as it allows you to tell it with the voice or tone that the main character uses.

Now let's take a look at the third person view. This will allow us to take the same story as before and place it in third person.

It was the best moment in her entire life. She felt herself freed from death's cold clutches and emerge from the blackness that was oblivion.

As she struggled to bring herself back to life slowly, she attempted to recollect her past and who she was.

She then opened her eyes and remembered.

The third person view is written in such a way that the main character's actions are being reported on to the reader. (She felt herself emerge... best moment of her entire life.

Most of you will agree that this piece of writing doesn't benefit from a change of perspective. It can, however, make things very different in certain cases. It can make the story seem less personal but it can also work well in many situations. If the story has more than one main character, third person perspective is great.

It doesn't matter if you choose third or first person writing, the point of view character is the person who will tell the story. His or her eyes, ears and emotions will dictate how the reader perceives the story.

Tensed

This chapter examines the main options for authors when choosing which tense in which to write. You can choose the past, which is the standard approach to storytelling and the one most commonly used. You could also choose to write your story in present tense. It has been increasingly popular in short story and novel writing over the past decade.

I'm sure that you already know the terms past tense and present tense. But just to make it clear, these are some examples of their use. Here's a short story excerpt in the past tense.

I entered the gift store with the intention of stealing. It wasn't expensive; it was a small, shiny trinket which would easily fit into my pocket. Then, I noticed who was behind it and my foolish, stupid plans to shoplifting vanished into thin air.

This is quite clear, doesn't it? The past tense of the extract is used to say: I entered, this would, I noticed, was sitting, crumbled into everything.

Here's the same excerpt in the present.

I am determined to steal anything when I enter the gift shop. It's nothing extravagant, but a small, shiny trinket I can easily slip into my wallet. Then, I realize who is behind it and my silly plans for shoplifting become a mirage.

It is amazing how it has changed. When I enter, it is standing and crumbling to nothing.

That's it. Isn't that easy? While the example I have used is in the first-person, it works equally well in both the present and future tense.

Advantages and drawbacks

It's easy to see why you would choose past tense rather than present, or vice versa. The reason is that reading stories in the past tense makes you feel you're actually reading about something that happened. It's like events are being described after they've occurred.

Stories written in present tense can create a sense that the story is happening right now, especially when it's combined with a first person perspective. The present tense can be likened to watching events unfold in real time when you read a story. You're there. It's all part of what you are doing. It works well in stories with suspense.

I've heard it also said that stories written with the present tense have a more literary quality. But I'm not sure if that's true. Let you decide.

According to my experience, flashbacks are the biggest problem with the use of the present tense in a story. Flashback cannot be written using the present tense because of its nature. As a result, you will find yourself jumping back and forth between the past, present, and the future. It can be quite distressing. According to me, stories that contain large portions of flashback are better written using the pluperfect time tense for flashbacks. (As explained in Chapter on Flashback).

Check the writing guidelines for any magazine that you intend to submit your story to. Some editors won't accept stories written using the present tense.

It's a good idea to experiment a bit if your writing is new. The story you wrote last Thursday might work well in the present. To make sure you don't forget the original story, save it and play around with the text. Change the tense to find out what effect it has. Also, experiment with your viewpoint. Your story may be written in the third-person. Be sure to save a copy. This way, you can quickly go back to the original version if it doesn't work.

It's amazing to see how a change in viewpoint or tense can affect the story's sound and feel. Test out all the options to determine which one works best. It will be obvious which one works best for the story that you are writing.

Let's talk about conflict now.

Conflict

Consider the following questions when you plan and begin to write your short story:

* What is the goal of your main character? What does your main character want?

* What motivates them to reach this goal? What is their motivation for pursuing this goal?

* What is preventing them from reaching their goal? What are the obstacles that

prevent them from achieving their goals? These are the issues that will create conflict within your stories.

The word conflict is often mentioned in the theory of writing. However, don't let that mislead your mind. Many new writers mistakenly believe that conflict must involve high drama or battle. This simply isn't true.

Let's have a look at synonyms for the word conflict to get a better understanding of what "conflict" might be.

* Battle

* Fight

* War

* Quarrel

* Argument

* Dispute

All of them sound confrontational and dramatic, but they are all true. However, there are many synonyms.

* Struggle

* Clash

* The Encounter

* Disagreement

*Difference

* Tension

These alternatives are not as confrontational or dramatic, but they're just as valid and are likely to be more frequent than conflicts in fiction writing.

You can think of conflict in this way: a barrier that stops your main character achieving his goal. If your story requires it, it can be a battle or an all-out conflict. However, it will often be less dramatic than the main character.

You could have conflict because of deep-seated emotions or beliefs. You could feel a fear or lack of commitment, anxiety, confidence, need to conform, or an underlying sense of resentment. These emotions or beliefs will prevent your protagonist achieving their goal.

No matter whether the drama is high-strung or less action-packed, the conflict will originate from:

* Within himself or herself

* conflict with another person, or

* A conflict with the circumstances (usually involves a situation that cannot be easily changed).

Conflict in fiction is simply the term for a problem or situation that the character must solve. The character must either succeed or fail on their own and grow or change as a consequence. Let's go back to Gently Does It. Now let us ask:

What was the main character's goal? What was she trying to achieve? Gently Does It suggests that Joanne's goal is to create a loving, stable relationship with her stepdaughters.

Why did she set out to accomplish this goal? What is her motivation to achieve this goal? Joanne is now in love with Will. She wants her marriage success and the home to be supportive and loving for her children.

What is holding her back from achieving her goals? What are her obstacles to achieving this goal? What's the conflict in the story Let's see, what do we think? Do you still have questions?

Conflict in the Gently Does It tale

Now, tell me: What did you think the conflict was. If you answered pineapple pizza and Ham, then this chapter is for you! Joanne's persistent food problems are a part of the conflict. However, Alice's inability or inability to accept Joanne as part of their lives is the main conflict. Alice has lost the mother she loved and is uncertain about Joanne's place in her life.

Joanne is also conflicted by her own desire to be perfect. Joanne feels insecure comparing herself to the mother of the children. The conflict can only be resolved when:

* Joanne recognizes she is not perfect but accepts it.

* Alice gains trust in her by letting it be known that she isn't trying to assume the role of 'mother'.

We know that the story's end doesn't mean the end is certain, but it gives us hope that things will get better for Joanne, Alice and their whole family.

This story is a reference to the fact that conflict does not need to be extremely dramatic or life-threatening. Gently Does It is over. Alice and Joanne both have learned valuable things about each other, which will help them in their future relationship. Although there will be occasional arguments about pizza and trivial things, the main conflict - Alice accepting Joanne into her role as stepmother - is over.

Writers of fantasy and thrillers may be able to create more dramatic conflict. The type of story that you are writing will determine the nature of the conflicts.

It doesn't really matter what type of conflict you have, as long there is enough. Without it your story won't be successful.

Making characters

Your readers need to sympathize or like the main character in order to enjoy your story. They need to know what motivates them and feel their actions are believable.

You will need characters that people can identify with. No one is perfect. Your characters shouldn't be. They should have flaws, weaknesses, and issues that readers can identify with.

It's important to remember that not all people are 'all good.' Everybody has good and bad qualities and human failures. If your protagonist seems too happy and cheerful, your readers might find it difficult to believe him.

The same goes for if you choose to create a villain in your fiction. However, it is important to remember that no one can be pure evil. Even the most evil person in the universe will have some redeeming traits. The antagonist doesn't even have to be evil. You only need them to hinder your main character's goal.

Character flaws may help to explain motivation and allow the reader to believe in the person they have created. We can understand the motivations behind your characters by revealing their flaws as long they don't interfere with the story.

Avoid stereotyping

Avoid stereotypical characters like the heroic soldier, woman in distress, strict schoolmistress, elderly grandmother, and other stereotypes. It is the characters that provoke emotions, whether fear, hatred, affection, laughter, love, disgust, and even horror, that make them great.

We won't even give a second thought to the plot if we fail to care about the characters.

Mannerisms are habits and traits

These elements are very useful in fiction. You can expect someone who leaves their shoes untied to fall over quite often. A nervous person may bite their nails and twist their hair. People's body language can reflect their emotions and even their personalities. Someone likely feels defensive if they cross their arms. This action reveals the character's emotions, without you needing to tell it directly.

Characters can be remembered by their mannerisms or other behaviors (irritating, not). Charlotte may clear her throat five times a day. Ben might spend hours picking at invisible fluff on his jacket sleeves. Take a look at what this tells you about the person.

It is a good idea to give each character a trait that guides their behavior and dictates their personality. It could be fear or worry, anxiety, greed or envy, as well as ambition and/or obsession. If someone is ruled by kindness, they will always place others first. On the other hand, someone who is ruled over by arrogance would always be first. This ruling trait will manifest itself in speech and actions. How would Mr. Arogant act in a crowded place? What if he was determined to keep pushing people aside? Probably. How would Mr Kind react in such a situation? Would he let himself be ignored by Mr Arrogant's? Remember, even Mr. Arogant may have some redeeming traits, as we said earlier. Maybe he has a great sense or humor, or he's a skilled sportsman that is loved by all his team-mates.

Your characters' habits, mannerisms and traits can be a powerful tool to help build trustworthiness and make them memorable. However, they shouldn't be repeated too often.

Your characters described

Sometimes it's the smallest details that readers will remember and relate to when you describe your characters. A brief description of your character is not necessary. It's not necessary to list every detail about your character, including their hair color, style, shape, weight, appearance, clothing, and speech, unless it is pertinent to the plot. It is much better to detail a little, perhaps something that sets the character apart from other characters. This could be their bright red hair and limp walking, or their soft sing-song voice.

It's difficult to convey a complete description of a character in short stories. Allow the reader to fill in the gaps by describing only one or two aspects.

Conceive your characters

Before you can begin to write about a character you need to have an idea. This is possible in many different ways. You can:

They should be based on real people that you know. However, it is important to not offend others. It is better to blend traits and attributes from different people than to create a person you can recognize.

Consider giving your fictional characters certain traits that you have. You can then emphasize those traits by making them an intrinsic part your character.

Play around with the idea of giving your protagonist traits and beliefs that are opposite to yours. This can be difficult but rewarding. You will be challenged by your imagination, and you may end up with some controversial or interesting characters.

Have fun! Spend time with people watching, especially in public places (train stations, airports bars, shops, etc.). Take note of how people act and walk. Also, pay attention to their speech patterns and expressions. Next, let your imagination do the rest.

Clothes maketh the man

Now let's think about how you might dress. People's clothes can reflect their outlook on life and circumstances. You can see the character of your character by looking at what they wear. Names are like clothes. They have associations and can make people seem like a certain kind of person. To take an example, which type of person do these clothing conjure for you?

* A leather jacket with ripped jeans

* A set of twins with pearls

* An ankle-length purple flowing, flowing skirt

* A tweed jacket paired with corduroy trousers

* A hand-knitted jumper.

The triggers will be used by all of us to create our characters and ideas based off individual experiences and associations.

You have a limited amount of words to describe your characters in a short story. Although it can help you create character, the reader doesn't have to know everything about your characters except that they are essential parts of the plot. It is enough to draw an impression by mentioning a unique piece of clothing, or an unusual accessory.

What's the point of a name?

The best way to make your fictional character more real is by choosing the right name.

While it may take time to find the right name for you, you'll soon be able recognize it. Once you settle on a name it will be hard to change later. But, keep in mind that editors can change names once stories are published. These are some things you should consider when choosing your name.

The sound and rhythm of the surname and the first name: Does it go well together? Or does it jar? Avoid using funny names, unless you are writing humour. In a romantic story, Eileen Marksworth would marry Charles Dover. You'd have a woman named Eileen Dover. For a gentler vibe, soft names like

Jenny and Susie, Helen and Terry, Jeremy and Jeremy are more appropriate. Max, Kurt and Max are a bit more serious than Nickki, Lana or Katrina. You should choose a name that suits your character. If you want your protagonist to be strong and virile, you wouldn't use the name Jim Postlethwaite. You could however choose James Waite.

Be sure that your chosen name is appropriate for the character you are choosing. Old-fashioned names may be back in style, but certain names instantly conjure up images of a particular age group. For example, Agnes, Maude Mavis Wendy Shirley Sharon Kylie. There are many websites that provide information on the origins and meanings for names. They also offer a way to check whether the name you choose is appropriate for your story. Visit babynames.co.uk/babynames.com.

Avoid using characters with identical names or names that start with the exact same letter. This will confuse readers and make tagging who is who difficult. You can also vary the length of the names of your characters to give more distinction (Tara or Geraldine for example, instead than Tara, Emma).

If you don't have to, keep your stories simple and avoid using unusual names.

The name of a person is often a clue to their heritage. There are obvious examples such as Ross McKenzie (of Scottish origin), or Patrick Donohue(of Irish origin), but there is also subtler names. If you go back to Jim Postlethwaite, a surname of this nature conjures up images that are reminiscent of the north of England. Williams, Davies (Jenkins), Jenkins, Rees, and Jones all give off a Welsh-inspired flavor.

Naming a character is not always as easy as one might think. It is difficult to know how a child's personality will develop when a baby is born. A fictional character will give you an idea of who they are and what their character traits are before you even conceive them. It is crucial that your fictional character's name matches the personality you wish to portray.

Pip from Charles Dickens' Great Expectations is one of the most memorable fictional characters. It fits him well and symbolizes that he is an individual who will grow from childhood to adulthood. Joy is a bright, happy character.

As I've mentioned, it's possible for the publishing editor to change the name of your character. A contemporary short story I wrote once featured Tim, a character that I had previously written about. He was not one of the main characters but I was surprised when the magazine published the story and discovered that his name has been changed to Wilf. Wilf, I mean, who else is Wilf these days. I was compensated enough for the story so I don't really complain. But, Tim will always be that character for me. This was how I met him, and that's where he'll remain.

Remember these points when you are creating characters to your first short story.

* Is the name appropriate to the age of your character

* How does your name look on the page? (Avoid any names that are too similar or clashing).

* How does the sound make it sound when it is read aloud (you may know how to pronounce it but will the reader?

* Does it reflect your character?

Once you've created a character and decided to set him up in a setting, it's important to reflect on the context.

Setting up and description

Fiction is characterized by description. It depicts the actions of the characters, their physical appearances, facial expressions and gestures as well as the setting in which they take place.

When describing characters, settings, and action in novels, novelists can go into greater detail. A short story writer will have fewer words available so descriptions must be more delicate. While descriptions must include sufficient detail and colour to define a character and create an atmosphere, you won't have time to add every little detail.

Describing people

I covered characterisation in Chapter 2. One of the best ways to develop characters is to describe them. You have plenty of words in a novel for this, but you don't have many words in a short story. Therefore, avoid giving too much detail about the character, such as their appearance and clothing.

There are some devices that you should avoid. For example, the one where your main character is staring at herself in a mirror admiring her long red locks. This approach is outdated and stale. It's better to leave the reader to determine how a character appears, rather than describing it in a complicated way.

There are other subtle ways you can describe characters. The best way to visualize characters is through the eyes of another person.

I watched from the beach as she stood in front of the water and I saw the wind blow red tendrils of hair across my face. She shoved them back, and I saw how angry she was.

Setting

Every story should be set somewhere. It doesn't have to take place on an exotic island. A single room is usually enough, but the setting has to be appropriate for your story.

It's okay to give a brief description about the place where your story is set, but don't make it workaday. Setting the scene doesn't require a long, boring paragraph. The setting can be made an integral part your story and done much more efficiently.

Do not feel pressured to explain every detail about a particular room or place. It's sufficient to mention some of the unique details that will make your scene memorable.

The setting you choose will be easily identifiable and help the reader visualize the scene. Without a backdrop, your characters will perform their roles in a vacuum.

Make sure you are specific

There are many different ways to describe a place, as well as how to paint it. You can convey a quick impression by using a variety of colours, shapes, light, and lighting, or you can describe something more in detail. To create emotion or atmosphere, you can also concentrate on one aspect of the scene.

A monochrome setting can be a great way to make something stand out. You could use light and dark in black and white. Next, add vivid colour to the background. Anita Shreve, author of the book, excels at this. Her books have beautiful descriptions and atmospheric settings. Sea Glass is her novel. Honora walks along the beach looking for a piece. Anita

Shreve explains the details of the tiny piece of glass and its colour. She said that it was green, pale and cloudy. This is similar to lime juice that has been squeezed in a glass. Shreve also talks about touch when she describes the glass's weathered, smooth look. Because of this, Shreve gives the glass an extra dimension and a sense that it is important.

While you can't give as much detail in a story, it can be more memorable and fun for the reader to be specific. Do not just state that something is "green", but also say it is "the colour of lime juice", or "emerald", or "the skin of Granny Smith apples". Be specific.

Keep in mind that you should not fill your prose completely with description. Mixing description with dialogue will keep your story moving.

Write using the five senses

Writers tend not to pay attention to the visual aspects of descriptions. We use words to describe colour, light, darkness, movement and shapes. Another sense used frequently by writers is sound. We talk about the wind moving through the trees and the whine of the car alarm. We mention bird song and children's laughter as well as the train's hum through a valley.

It is the senses of touch, taste and smell that we tend to forget. These senses can sometimes be used to produce vivid and memorable details. These descriptions can also be enhanced by using visual or auditory references. Consider, for instance, how the sea sounds as it runs on a pebbled sandy beach. Or the white foam rising at the water's edges. Why not also mention the sea salty smell or taste? These sensual references can transport your reader to that scene as if they were actually there.

It's possible to go overboard with writing techniques. Be subtle. There are ways to add some senses. But you don't need to include them all every time. Select the ones that are clear and original to improve the quality and clarity of your story.

Sight: Give the readers enough information to allow them to see what your story is about. If it is a character, describe what they look like, how they walk or stand.

A character's facial expressions are a reflection of their mood. The expressions of a character's face reflect their mood.

When you describe a scene or place, please indicate whether it is day, night or dark, inside or outside. Is your story set on the South Coast of England? What is different about it from beaches in California, Spain, and Wales? What are the unique aspects of your setting?

A short story can give you an impression of a place. You don't have to include every detail.

Sound: Close your eye and take a trip to your imaginary (or real) location. Then, ask yourself the question: What would you hear? Traffic? A dog barking? The indecipherable banter of a crowd Farm animals? Bird song?

Be specific if farm animals can be heard. Mention the lowing and bleating of sheep. Do not just claim that you can hear bird songs. Give a description of the sound that an owl makes or of a robin singing. Be specific to avoid being bland.

Smell: Is your character surrounded by car fumes when they're in a big city? Are they able to smell the earthy aroma of a forest when they're in the country? Oder the smell of wood smoke wafting from a nearby house? Close your eyes, and imagine yourself in that setting. You can use your imagination. Use your imagination.

Taste: A restaurant can offer a variety of wonderful aromas, along with texture and flavor. I am always drawn to garlic's aroma. What is it about garlic that appeals to the most?

If you want to convey the atmosphere of the area, mention local foods and drinks.

The taste of food doesn't always have to be limited. Water is not something that tastes very well. However, if your character has been sitting on a hillside for hours and has not had a drink in a while, then a glass or two of chilled water might taste great. Fear has its own taste, just like kisses. People who have been punched in the face will feel pain. They may touch their damaged teeth or taste blood.

Touch: Textures vary, and they can be used to great advantage in description. Consider how the sand feels between the toes while you stroll along the beach. It is quite a pleasant sensation, isn't you think? However, think about what happens when you return home after washing your feet and still feel the grains between your toes. Irritating, isn't it?

When you were a kid, imagine how it felt to fall onto a rough tarmac track. As your skin slid to a halt you would feel it rubbing against your skin. Your hands would feel numb where you used them to brace for your fall. Most likely, bits of grit were embedded in your skin. You then felt the sting of the disinfectant after your grazed leg was cleaned up. The touch is all that matters.

This principle can be applied to your own writing

If you've started writing your first story already, you can now read it through and review which senses have been used. By combining, you can add additional detail to the writing.

* sight

* sound

* Smell

* taste

* touch.

Decide which one of these details creates the most striking image. These details can be added to your existing description to add uniqueness to your piece.

Get started with your story

Before we proceed, I would like to encourage you (if not already) to start writing your very first short story. Now that you know most of the techniques needed to build your story, it's time you put them into practice.

Writing dialogue

A story that is short will be more interesting if there is good dialogue. A story without dialogue will be like an apple pie without cream, or rhubarb with no custard.

Three functions are performed by dialogue in fiction:

* It contains information about your characters.

* It advances the story by providing the reader with information about the plot.

* It can add depth and realism into your story.

You should make sure that every dialogue you write has at least one (or more!) of the three functions listed above. If it doesn't, it's redundant and should be cut from your story.

Realistic dialogue

Dialog in fiction should be understood as a form of dialogue. It sounds like real speech, but it isn't.

You can think about it. Real life has many pitfalls. People talk in half sentences and insert lots of "erms" and "ahs" into conversations. Sometimes, we will even stop mid-sentence. There is also a lot more unnecessary waffle than would be necessary for a short story. If you were to record two friends talking and then transcribe it, it would likely be dull and slow moving. Fiction is about cutting to the chase. Use dialogue to tell a story or establish character.

A lot can be attributed to the way people talk. Through speech, personality can be evoked.

* What is being said, and

* This is how it should be said.

An example of this is a person who is arrogant. His speech could be long, loud, and self-absorbed. Shy people may not be able to make long speeches. Their voices may also sound soft and uncertain. The voice of your characters will reflect your character's age, background, personality, and many other factors. A person's intelligence or age may be expressed in their vocabulary. An accent or dialect can tell you a lot about where they are from.

Fiction: Accents and dialects

Use accents or dialects sparingly in your stories if you want to reflect a local culture. If your prose is too long, it will make it difficult for the reader to understand and could even lead to a rejection.

D H Lawrence uses dialogue sections written in an East Midlands dialect in Sons and Lovers and a number of his other novels and poems. Here's a quick excerpt from Sons and Lovers. Arthur Morel is talking to his girlfriend. It's not an easy book to read.

She would occasionally smoke with her husband. Sometimes, she would only take a few inhale of his cigarette. She reached for her cigarette and he responded, "Nay," one night. "Nay. Tha doesna. I'll gie thee an occasional smoke kiss if there's a mind," he replied. "Well, an'tha'lt hae a whiff," said he, "along with wi' t 'kisse."

I'm from East Midlands and find that it is much easier than the majority of people. But I still struggled to understand this book. Although the novel is wonderful, there are many who struggle with the dialect.

You can communicate accents or dialects in fiction best by not using them too much, maybe by using a unique phrase or slang that is related to the area you are from.

Take for instance the possibility that people from different parts might share some ideas:

One character might respond, "She's gorgeous!"

Someone from the south might respond, "She is a lovely gal."

An east coaster might reply, "Aye! She's a bonny lass."

Someone from Scotland might respond, "She's a fine shee lassie."

This is not the place to stereotypize. It's not a good idea to assume that people speak the same way no matter where they live.

To be subtle is the most sensible approach. One example is to mention a character's accent in the story. A foreign accent can be displayed in the way your characters construct sentences.

It is important to ensure the dialogue is clear when portraying an accent.

Action in dialogue

Breaking up the dialogue with action is a great habit to adopt. This is not always necessary but can speed up the pace, especially for short fiction. Consider this example:

Katy started her ironing while she was trying to figure out what was bothering her daughter. She lifted a shirt and rolled the iron along one sleeve.

"You're very quiet, Ella. "What's up, Ella?

"Nothing."

"Are you sure? It's not unusual for you to be so glum."

Ella answered, switching between TV channels. "Leave my alone," Ella said.

Imagine how sparse that same conversation would appear if we were only reading it in isolation. Even though the actions and tasks are not exciting, Katy's and Ella's daily lives make it more real and believable.

Speech tags

A word on speech tags: he said, she responded, he shouted, so on.

Many writers want to be creative and include variety in their writing. Once in a while, the large number of tags can be distracting. It then becomes irritating and comical.

The best way to approach the situation is to use 'said' in all cases. It is subtle and almost indistinct to the reader, so it does not interfere with the dialogue.

Other tags can be used to make things more interesting, such as shouted, asked, responded, or shouted. However, this should only be done when needed. Sometimes, you won't need to add a tag. Let's take a look at this example. These are the middle line from that extract.

"You're very quiet, Ella. What's going on?

"Nothing."

"Are you sure? It's not unusual for you to be so glum."

It is easy to see who is speaking, so speech tags don't need to be used. If you have a lot of dialogue, it is important that the reader can track who is speaking. Add a tag for every four or five lines, if needed, to ensure that they are able to track who is speaking.

Avoid the blunders of saying things like these:

She smiled, "I am so happy," Or

He grinned.

You can also speak. You can also ask questions. You can also reply to questions. You can't smirk, smile, or frown at any question. It is possible to do all of these things simultaneously and still talk, but the words come from your vocal chords. Not your expressions.

You can use facial expressions and actions to convey the mood of a character. But you need to use them properly.

She smiled. Or

He grimaced. "It is agony," he stated.

It is a great way to increase your skills in dialogue. Read widely, keep writing, and read aloud your work to yourself, your spouse, your partner, or a friend. Speaking out loud can help you discover if your dialogue works.

Thoughts

There are many ways you can express your thoughts through fiction. Here are some examples.

She thought it better not to say anything.

She thought I'd better not tell anyone.

Better she didn't speak at all.

All of the examples above are acceptable. Some writers prefer to write thoughts like dialogue.

She thought "I'd rather not say anything", she said.

Personally, I find speech marks that are used with thought confusing. I have trouble determining if the words were spoken out loudly unless the tag is checked. Technically speaking, there's nothing wrong with this last example. Some stories do use speech markers for thought. But my personal recommendation? To avoid using speech marks if you can. It's better to use one or more of the examples I presented:

She believed that it was better to keep silent.

She thought I'd better not tell anyone.

It's better she didn't speak at all.

Let me end with a word of advice for dialogue

Some people have a natural ability to write dialogue. Others need to put in the effort to make it sound perfect. If I had one thing to say, it would be that you make sure that your characters don't talk the same. Your characters should have their own unique voice.

A person's speech pattern, favourite words, style or voice can make them stand out and help build character. Remember, it's all in what they say and how.

Flash Fiction and Short Stories - Elements

A story has a beginning middle and an ending. Flash fiction is no exception. A short story should only take 30 minutes to read. The reader shouldn't have time to go through any backstory before diving into the main points of the story. The reader should not be required to read lengthy back stories even when a novel is full length. In a longer novel, however, the reader may be willing and able to tolerate more backstory without complaining than with shorter stories.

Flash fiction is traditionally minimalist in its approach. This style relies heavily on unexpected endings and clever plot twists. They are becoming more common in short stories.

Writing a 1,000-word summary of the beginning, middle, or end can be challenging. Writing flash is a way to get your point across quickly. While this can work well with short stories, you don't necessarily have to be so careful when choosing words for a short story.

Many writers see their craft from a different angle by writing shorter stories. When you take a look at your own style, you will realize how much you must sacrifice to write a compelling story in such a limited space. You must get back to basics to ensure that every word counts.

Flash fiction can be useful for both experienced and new authors. Flash fiction helps you learn to prioritize and gets to the core of your story. Flash fiction can also be used as a way to outline a larger piece.

Let's examine the four main elements of an excellent story.

Setting is the location of the action. Flash fiction shouldn't exceed one sentence. You can add details to the dialogue. Sometimes, the title can be all that is needed to determine the setting.

Characters are only allowed to operate in the given setting. In flash fiction, you shouldn't have more that two, maybe three, characters.

They simply don't have enough space. It is important to remember that characters do not have to be humans or animated. Imagine the conflict that occurs between a block or ice with a dark colored stone on the top. Now imagine what happens after it goes down and the block freezes again.

Conflict can be anything from a disagreement to keep the reader interested. It could be verbal, mental, or physical. There is no need for tension between your villain and your hero.

Resolution is the end of the conflict. It's okay to use small words in flash fiction. A miracle that saves your protagonist is not necessary. However, a satisfying resolution to an existing conflict can make the reader happy. Flash fiction is a popular genre that uses surprise endings. This is because it's more fun for both the author and the reader. You shouldn't surprise readers too much, even when there is a twist. You want your readers to be able to say "aha" and "ah, ofcourse" with a happy reaction, not feeling foolish or stupid for not seeing the ending coming.

Flash fiction does not represent an idea for writing a story. It's not a snippet of everyday life. It's a whole story. The main difference is that it shows change. A vignette does not usually depict change, it simply shows the current status of something. Flash fiction and short stories must reflect change in the protagonist or antagonist.

Although it is possible to use a typical plot, you can add a twist by ending the story.

Strategies for Flash Fiction & Short Stories

Many of the strategies you can use to write flash fiction and short stories are very similar to those used in writing novels. However, space limitations quickly become a problem with flash fiction and short stories which can limit your options.

Start by exploring smaller ideas. The serialization of a larger piece of work is one great use of shorter stories. Each small piece of the larger issue needs to be read on its own. However, if you handle it well, you can make each story stand alone. Each can help your customers purchase the next series - even though each story ends with a cliffhanger. You can think about the way that some old television serials were made. Even though you could watch one episode and be satisfied, the episodes often left you wanting more. You would return to the next episode the week after. Another way is to use the same characters across multiple stories. Imagine a "day of" treatment.

Eliminate the backstory. This is a great idea, even in a novel. It's not necessary to go through many pages before you see the action. It is crucial to get straight to the action, even if you have flashy stories. If you have any backstory, it is important to get it out of your first paragraph.

Start with action. This is important with shorter stories as well. Do not tell more than is necessary. These are all examples of reasonable descriptions: "The window burst from the concussion external", "Two people are running from an alleyway", "I woke up seconds before the blast", etc. Don't over-describe. Allow the reader to complete the details.

One image is all that you need. The more elements you have, then the stronger your story can be. Draw a picture. A picture is worth a thousand letters, but it shouldn't take you that many words just to paint a picture in the minds of your readers.

A little mystery goes along a long way. Your reader will be interested in your story and kept guessing the whole time. This will entice them to the end. Keep them guessing. They should get a reward or a solution when they finish.

A common story can be used to save words. You can use historical events or famous scenes from literature. Don't use obscure material. Your reader might not be able make the inferences you want.

A twist is a way to add some excitement at the end. Because you don't have enough words to describe how a long and devastating plot has affected your characters, flash fiction, as well as short stories, often uses a twist in the end. Flash fiction is often reduced to a punch line at end.

Don't tie things up with a little bow. Make room for the next chapter or adventure. It is best to leave the issue in its current form, but open up for discussion. There's always the possibility of your heroine surviving, even if her story ends in tragedy. What will happen next? Purchase the next installment of this series... Serializing will build a following and bring you great money.

The shortest flash fictions are like a flashlight. They are only for a brief moment, providing light for a brief period of time and then they disappear quickly. Even though a story may have a twist ending or a beginning, middle, and end, it can still be a complete story with only 55 words. Sometimes, even less. While flash fiction can be written in as little as seven words by some people, that is too small for my liking.

Flash fiction captures what a story is all about, and a moment in time. It's straight-forward, simple, and direct. The subject is the main focus. The background is typically only briefly described. If it's present, the reader will assume or create it.

Flash fiction has very little time for description or detail. For the reader to fill in any gaps, you will need to rely on their experiences. Dialogue-driven stories can be used to quickly develop character, conflict, and action. Strong active verbs should be used and there should not be any linking verbs or adjectives. You can create your characters without having to give too much detail by using effective dialogue.

Like longer pieces, you must be aware of setting, character as well conflict and resolution. These elements may appear naturally in many longer works. But with flash fiction, it can be more challenging to include them all before you run out space. Conventional writing doesn't allow for many short sentences. Flash fiction makes it possible. They attract attention, convey meaning using their punctuation and can write entire paragraphs with just one word. They make great hooks.

Here are some tips to help when writing flash.

Write fast. Editing is the best way to ensure that grammar is not an issue. Fill at most a half-page, then count the words, fix grammar, and then you can read it aloud. If you're having a good time, continue until you run out of words, then count the number and fix it. Does it include the elements of Setting up, Conflict and Resolution? Does it create change?

Edit. Edit. Eliminate redundant adjectives. You will have tight, active sentences which are the heart of flash fiction.

Let dialogue do it. With as few tags possible, write an all-dialog story. The dialogue should describe the characters and create tension.

Avoid cliche flash. There are several topics to avoid. Some examples include stories about a writer or "it wasn't a dream" They are overused and misused in many fiction types, especially flash.

If you are writing flash fiction and your story is finished, you can simply stop. It's a good idea to write a short story.

Write your short story

Get started:

A few things you should consider when writing a short story. These questions will allow you to understand the story and help you plan your next steps. These questions can also be used to help you write.

First, look at your protagonist and decide what it is that you want. This must be something meaningful and concrete. This is a simple way to find out "who's my protagonist and what do they want?" Most likely, that is all you really require.

When the story starts, ask your protagonist what morally significant actions he has already taken toward the goal. These are not necessary to detail through backstory, but they should be kept in mind. You can also use them to help you understand your protagonist's motivations. Morally significant does mean your characters are not necessarily "good" or on right side of law. What is important is that they have made a conscious decision to make the best of what happened to them, rather than being victims of circumstances.

Ask what unexpected results will increase the emotional energy in the story. These consequences must directly relate to the protagonists' efforts to reach their goal.

How do setting, dialogue and tone aid in telling the story? Avoid giving away unnecessary information. It's generally not helpful to describe a journey scene when moving from one location to the next, unless something crucial happens along the way. Dialogue tags must be descriptive and give information about a subject. Tags such "smirked", 'bubbled', or "chortled," are more effective that "said happily".

What morally important choice will your protagonist make towards the end of the story's conclusion? This must be something your reader will enjoy and surprise you. If your reader is not interested in the protagonist's decision, then you have lost them somewhere in the story. The ending should have a twist so the reader can understand it.

Writing flash fiction and stories can be as difficult as any other type of writing. There are some things you can do to make it easier. You can save ideas by keeping a notebook or journal. Writing on a daily basis (or at least every day) helps to keep you on track and allows your brain to work efficiently on the writing craft. Keep your environment in mind. Take notes wherever you can. Note the extraordinary, strange, strange, and irrational tales you hear. Then, use them for yourself. These stories can be used to expand your understanding of human nature. Read. Read as many books as you can. It keeps your brain active. Reading fiction from other authors can help you subconsciously connect different writing styles to different genres. You can even read nonfiction to help you come up with ideas for fictional stories. Imagine "what if ...."". If you take a position that is contrary to common knowledge, you will discover many potential fiction themes.

Your first paragraph

The first sentence of any short story, as with all modern writing, should grab the reader's attention. You should start with tension and immediacy. Don't waste time wafflering about in short stories. A short story must be close to the end.

Create your characters

It is crucial to have a deep understanding of your character, just as you would with any other form of fiction. You will be able communicate a fully realized, multifaceted character to the reader. Before you write any substantial portions of your short story, you should have a basic outline about each of your characters. A character development checklist is used for all my fictional characters. I also use a world planning checklist to keep track and monitor the environment where my characters live. This is especially important when a short story evolves into a longer story. With this, I can make sure that my characters and the environment are consistent from one story after another. To write, I use a laptop. Lately, I have been creating two files for each novel or story. One is a list of character development checklists. The other is the actual book. You can also store ideas and other bits of information in the support file. I sometimes drag paragraphs out of the story file into the support file as I write. This allows me to refer back later. I typically name them Working-Title.doc and Working-Title-

Support.doc so I can easily find them. Final versions of Working-Title.doc are shortened to Title.doc and Title-Final.doc.

In addition to the obvious elements like name, age, gender, occupation, ethnicity and appearance, there are a few more aspects of character I like to outline upfront. Although this does not mean that I make it an ongoing project, it helps me to visualize and feel the character's feelings before I start writing. Although you may be able to visualize these details, you won't get to know the characters as well as your reader if they don't know anything beyond what you have revealed in Appearance, Action and Speech.

An appearance provides a visual representation of your character. Are they fussy, tidy, messy, tall or short?

Your character will be shown through your actions.

The dialogue you use will define your character. Be careful not to let your character only announce important plot details. The old saying, "show don't Tell" is just as applicable here as it is anywhere else in the writing world.

Thought lets you take the reader inside your character's mind and allow them to see their thoughts. But, don't take it too far, as you could lose the tempo, and even your reader.

Point of view

Point of view, as with all fiction, refers to the narration of the story in the third person, second, or first person. It is important to know who will tell the story and how much information can be revealed by the narrator. Flash fiction, or short stories, is less important than long feature length novels. This is because there are fewer chances to change the story's viewpoint and not confuse your reader.

First Person

Many stories are written in first person. The story is told from the viewpoint of "I", which is the protagonist. However, the narrator may be directly affected by the events unfolding or a secondary character. This story is often preferred by beginning authors as it is the easiest to create. The reader is more likely to identify with the protagonist because they are writing it from their point of view. Therefore, the reader feels the emotions and takes on the characters' actions. Romance stories tend to be written in the first person. The reader and the author are usually in the first person. They share a series of secrets with the character, which allows them to become one another. Be careful not to get bogged down in telling. This could limit the reader's connection with other characters.

There are some things that a first-person narration should not say. You shouldn't give descriptions of bodily parts or angles they wouldn't normally see. Or awkward statements that may indicate something the person doesn't know.

Directness is a benefit because it allows the reader to see the story from the author's perspective; voice because of the unique and appealing ways the characters talk can add to the story; intimacy because the reader can get to know the narrator simply by listening to him.

First-person disadvantages are limited scope and limited voice. The narrator can only know what the protagonist knows. He will not know what people around him see or think. He doesn't see what's happening beyond his immediate area. This affects the amount of information that the reader is able to see. This is because the voice must be representative of the character's age or mental state. It can sometimes be difficult to withhold important information. It's not always easy to keep information secret if the narrator knows something you don't want the reader know.

When you restrict your story to the viewpoint of a specific character, readers will be more emotionally and strongly attached to him.

First-person plural narration, a unique form of first-person fiction, is another example. To tell the story, the narrator uses a word called "we". This viewpoint is often difficult to master successfully.

Second Person

Second person is when the story is told directly and to "you", with the reader participating in the action. In instruction, the use of second person is common. However, it is not often used in short stories and flash fiction. Fiction often uses the second person to bring readers into the actual scene, so they can see all possibilities. However, placing your characters in a concrete environment that makes sense to them is essential to their understanding of the details. This viewpoint is more effective in longer fictions because you have more time.

Second person fiction presents a problem in that it is difficult to use without appearing contrived and without defying common sense. Because the viewpoint tells a reader what to do it can lead to negative reactions from readers to things they wouldn't normally do. This viewpoint works better in nonfiction books.

Third Person

The third-person point of view is related to "it", "she", or "he". The perspective of the third person narration can be limited (reporting from only one character) or omniscient (reporting all the information about the characters and revealing any necessary details to move the story forward). The third person perspective allows your narrator to take sides, be as transparent or even challenge you (which is often called the "unreliable and reliable narrator" approach). If you want to examine the thoughts and motivations, you can use the third person omniscient viewpoint. You must make transitions between characters so that your reader doesn't get lost. While a third person's limited point can allow for intimate character perceptions, you will need to manage their absence from other scenes. Or shift point to make your story more coherent. In short stories, it is often difficult to shift points of view frequently because there is not enough space or time.

A third person can have the ability to be anywhere at once and see all that is happening. The third person omniscient, third person narrator is able to give the reader unlimited visions and knowledge related to the characters.

Meaningful dialogue

Simply stated, dialogue is the language your characters use to communicate with each other or themselves. This is no different to other forms of fiction. However, the way your characters speak is very important in flash fiction and short stories. Every change in speaker should result a new paragraph. Each bit of dialogue will therefore be in its own paragraph. It is generally not necessary to identify the speaker or tag dialogue when having a conversation between two characters in a short story. If there are only two characters present in a scene and dialogue has been passing back and forth, the reader will be able to follow the conversation exactly as if they were watching or participating in a real conversation.

For flash fiction and short stories, dialogue tags are often used less than for longer stories. You should focus more on creating and using stronger dialogue. Next, you need to explain how tags can be used to help with dialogue. Moderation is crucial to eliminating dialogue tags, just as any other piece of advice. You can avoid telling your reader what is going by using meaningful dialogue tags or labels. It is possible to infer your characters' mental state by using inference. You can describe a detail that conjures in the reader an image of your character's mental condition. But, a little bit can go a long way.

Ask yourself why the reader is interested in a particular detail.

Setting and context

Setting is a combination of many elements. These include time, place and context. These elements are what determine the location of the plot. You must incorporate the setting and characters with the plot to create an engaging story. Although you need enough information to help your reader visualize the scene, only the essential details are necessary to tell the story. Extraneous information can be distracting or have little impact on the story. If there was something else about the process you wanted to highlight to your readers, you wouldn't describe it as a step-by–step procedure of going into the garage and setting up the mirror.

When describing a setting, you should use at least one sense. Your descriptions of setting should not be limited to information such as population statistics, weather conditions, and distances to destinations. Instead, give descriptive details that allow the reader to feel the place as your characters.

Establish the plot

Plot describes the main events in your story. It is the storyline. The action. Plot can be used to set the scene and show the key turning points. It also helps you decide what happens to the characters towards the end. It's a series of events designed to reveal the dramatic, emotional, and thematic meaning of your story. Your next short story will be more interesting if you understand the story elements and how characters' actions impact the reader's perception.

In your opening, you need a hook. A hook is something that grabs the attention of the reader immediately. If you don't have the time or patience to write a lengthy backstory, then start with action in your first sentence. This tension, or conflict, is what creates the story's beginning. Tension is created when there is opposition between the main character and other external or internal forces. The balance between the opposing forces can help keep the reader interested and guessing at the ending. There are many conflict options for your protagonist to encounter: against another person, against nature or technology or society, God, or against themselves. There will be conflict throughout the story. This could be an internal conflict that the character is facing, or it could be an external conflict.

There are many different ways you can create or show conflict in your story.

You can use mystery to tell your reader what you are up to, without giving away everything.

Empowerment can be defined as the willingness to accept and respect both sides' points of view.

Progression refers to the ability to increase or intensify the obstacles faced by your protagonist.

Causality means that you hold your fictional characters accountable for their actions more than real people. Characters who make mistakes often pay and, at least in the fiction world, they often reap the benefits.

You can surprise readers with enough complexity to prevent them from predicting the outcomes of your story far ahead.

Empathy is a way to encourage readers to identify with your characters, or with situations that resonate with their emotions, no matter how unpleasant they may be.

The ability to see the bigger picture can reveal much about human nature.

The universality principle can be used to present a struggle most readers find meaningful.

When you are convincing readers that the outcome is important for someone they care about, high-stakes scenarios can be used. Many stories are trivialized because of low stakes and trivial clashes among characters.

Exposition can be used within your story to provide background information that allows your readers to understand the character's actions. But you don't want to use too much exposition.

It is possible to use complications to create one or more problems that prevent a character reaching their desired goal. These complications can be interesting to the story, and they allow you to better develop your character in the mind.

Transitions can be described as mental images, symbols, or dialogue that join paragraphs or scenes together. Your readers will be able to follow your transitions easily so they don't become confusing.

Flashback can be used to recall an event that took place before the flash fiction takes place. It is only rarely used in flash fiction or short stories.

Climax marks the peak of increasing action in a story. Following the climax, there is falling action. This can allow the reader to pause and reflect on the actions that led up to the climax. The turning point or most dramatic moment in a story is called climax. This is usually near the end of short stories. It might be a recognition or decision. The character finally sees or understands what is needed. In one sense, this is when the "worm" turns and the bad guys get their desserts. Timing is critical when it comes to the climax. Timing is critical. If the climax happens too early, readers may expect a different, more powerful climax. If they don't, they will be unhappy with the story. If the climax occurs too late in a story, readers may become impatient. The character might seem slow, unresponsive or unintelligent.

Resolution is the process by which an external or internal conflict is resolved. This revelation is not meant to be a "moral of a story" or a final act that has a twist. The reader can decide what the final actions should be. If you present a clear and concise resolution at end of story, it will make your job easier. Short fiction is hard to resolve. Your story should only show how the characters are evolving or if they see things differently. You let the reader decide what the story means if you leave the resolution up to them. If it is resolved, you give the reader a clear and concise outcome. Sometimes the resolution can be parallel to the beginning. The resolution is often a similar point to the original scene or situation. This is not uncommon for serialized stories. When the resolution leads to a monologue the protagonist makes a statement either internally or externally which provides the resolution. Sometimes, resolution ends with dialogue between characters who discuss what they have seen or done. Sometimes resolution may be found in the presentation of symbolic or literal images that contain details that create an image in readers' minds.

Beyond the story

Because they are not well-marketed, this is often the last element of flash fiction and short story success. This is what i call the "hook to the next book". This is where your story can be carried forward to another episode. Or, you can carry your protagonist to another scenario that can entertain your readers. For novels, this is usually the first chapter. Because of the small space in short stories, this is often done by giving the first paragraph with a "sales pitch", a sentence and embedded link to next book. This is an effective way to build a readership and increase sales for your series of short stories. Even if the follow-up material isn't written yet, as long your reader asks "What if?" it can be a good start to the next installment. Tomorrow is always another day. This gives you another opportunity to entertain your readers.

Additional notes

There are some additional warnings to be aware of when you write flash fiction or short stories. These will allow you to create your story more easily and ensure that your readers understand it. While some of these may look familiar as we've already discussed them in this book, they are worth repeating.

Stick to one viewpoint and use few characters. There are simply too many characters to keep track of, and you don't have the time or space for more than two.

Your story's time limit should be kept to a minimum. While some authors might jump around in time, your chances of success are greatest if you keep the story short. It is not realistic to try and cover the entire life of a character in only a few thousand words. It is also almost impossible to do it in less that 1,000 words. A short story is a concise and effective way to cover a lot of ground in a relatively short time. It could be as brief or long as one incident in the life or day of your protagonist.

Make sure you are selective in your editing. All that you keep should be used to advance the story or to build your character. This is just like regular fiction, but more so for short stories or flash fiction.

Be consistent with the conventions of story structure. But, keep in mind that you have the ability to break the rules when it is appropriate. Telling your story is the most important part.

World building should not be slow and tedious. A novel allows you to go on for pages about your imaginary world and how it can be reached faster than light travel. Your story must be short and concise.

Believe that there's more to the world than just what is happening in their immediate surroundings. While you won't be able to spend hundreds of pages building worlds, you should have enough details to convince us that there's more to the world than we see. It's like old cowboy movies where the fake storefronts and houses are compared to real stores or homes. It's possible to see small parts of your virtual world that don't necessarily correspond with your characters' obsessions.

Your characters don't have to be perfect. They will occasionally make mistakes. They should have some baggage. Everybody in the real-world has.

It's important to get into the details right from the beginning. However, you shouldn't divulge your plot in more than the first paragraph. Your characters will have more time to deal with the issue if you let them freak out in the very first sentence. It is important to remember that if you are writing series, the same place in which your characters start can become boring. Good short stories keep the reader guessing while keeping them engaged and allowing you to get to grips with the characters.

www.ingramcontent.com/pod-product-compliance
Lightning Source LLC
Chambersburg PA
CBHW050412120526
44590CB00015B/1930